THE ALTAR FIRE

THE
ALTAR FIRE

REFLECTIONS ON THE SACRAMENT
OF THE EUCHARIST

OLIVE WYON

SCM PRESS LTD
BLOOMSBURY STREET LONDON

First published 1954
Reprinted 1954
Reprinted 1956
Reprinted 1963

Printed in Great Britain by
Billing and Sons Limited
Guildford and London

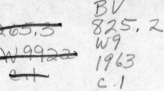
PREFACE

THIS BOOK is not another 'manual' for the use of regular communicants. Rather, it has grown out of an increasing concern for the many people (whether 'church-goers' or not) who are perplexed and uncertain about fundamental Christian beliefs and practices. Nowhere does this uncertainty work out more disastrously than in connection with the central act of Christian worship: the Eucharist. This book is therefore offered to all who want to enter more fully and deeply into their great Christian heritage.

The title, *The Altar Fire*, is an allusion to the Jewish Temple worship, and to the ever-burning altar fire (cf. Lev. 6.8-13). Fire is a frequent religious symbol. Fire is new life, and the fire-bringer is the Mediator, who brings new life from heaven to earth. Early Christian writers often applied this term to Christ: 'Thou who art all fire, have mercy upon me'.

The debt I owe to many writers will be evident. But I would like to express my very warm gratitude to those who have helped me directly in various ways: to the members of my family circle, especially Mrs. Lily Broadbent and Deaconess Hetty Wyon; for criticism, suggestions and advice I am also greatly indebted to my friends the Reverend C. H. Dodd, D.D., the Reverend J. W. Stevenson, M.A., and the Right Reverend Kenneth Warner, Bishop of Edinburgh. The Reverend Mark Wilson, M.A., has kindly read the proofs. My thanks are also due to Messrs. Faber and Faber Ltd. for permission to quote from *The Divine Realm*, and to the Society for Promoting Christian Knowledge for permission to quote from *A Procession of Passion Prayers*.

OLIVE WYON

St. Colm's College
   Edinburgh
      October 1953

CONTENTS

		PAGE
Preface		5
PROLOGUE: THE UPPER ROOM		9
1	THE SIGNIFICANCE OF THE SACRAMENT	13
2	WORSHIP AND THE EUCHARIST	22
3	'IN REMEMBRANCE OF ME'	33
4	THE SACRIFICIAL CENTRE	42
5	THE ROYAL PRIESTHOOD (*a*)	55
6	THE ROYAL PRIESTHOOD (*b*)	65
7	HOLY COMMUNION	80
8	THE COMMUNICANT	95
9	THE EUCHARIST IN THE WORLD CHURCH	107
EPILOGUE: 'UNTIL HE COME'		115
NOTE 1	The Character of the Last Supper	121
2	The Word 'Sacrament'	122
3	Sacrificial Rites	123
4	Self-Examination in the Light of the Beatitudes	124

For I received of the Lord that which also I delivered unto you, how that the Lord Jesus in the night in which he was betrayed took bread; and when he had given thanks, he brake it, and said, This is my body, which is for you: this do in remembrance of me. In like manner also the cup, after supper, saying, This cup is the new covenant in my blood: this do, as oft as ye drink it, in remembrance of me. For as often as ye eat this bread, and drink the cup, ye proclaim the Lord's death till he come.

I Corinthians 11.23-26 (R.V.)

THE UPPER ROOM

DARKNESS had fallen on the city of Jerusalem. The seething crowds who had jostled each other all day long in the narrow streets and in the Temple courts had disappeared: some to their lodgings in the city for their evening meal; and thousands more to camp out under the stars. Across the Valley of the Kidron gleams of light among the trees on the Mount of Olives showed where families were sitting at supper round their camp-fires.

Here and there, within the city, a belated traveller was still out on the street. Presently, through the City Gate came a small group of young men. The gate-keeper looked at them curiously; turning to a companion lounging near by he said: 'Look! That's Him!' The man looked after the group in some bewilderment and then turned to his friend and said: 'What do you mean? Who's that?' Scornfully the gate-keeper answered: 'Why, who *could* it be but Jesus of Nazareth?'

Meanwhile Jesus and His friends were walking swiftly along the quiet street, and they were soon out of sight. Once or twice one or another would look round to see whether they were being followed. With a sigh of relief they said quietly: 'No, not a soul in sight!' Soon they came to a door in a high wall. A slave answered their knock, and in a moment they were upstairs in a large Upper Room, well lit and furnished. Supper was ready; but the friends of Jesus were not.

Only a few days before this fateful Thursday,[1] two of them—James and John—had begged for seats of honour in the Kingdom they thought Jesus was about to set up. The others were very angry with them. However, the quarrel seemed to have been smoothed over; but every now and again their smouldering irritation would break out in hot and angry words. On the long walk up from Jericho to Jerusalem they had been arguing hotly

[1] See Note 1, p. 121.

among themselves: 'Which of us is the greatest?' Even now their tempers were still irritated; their feet were dusty, and their hands unwashed.

As they went into the Upper Room they noticed that there was no slave present to wash the feet of the guests. But the basin, the large water-jug, and the clean towel were there, near the door. In the absence of a slave it was the duty of the youngest member of the party to do this service for the others. But these young men were still too full of their recent arguments, and too disturbed, to offer this act of courtesy. So they ignored the need for cleansing, and went forward into the room.

The preliminary part of the meal was already on the table; after a brief blessing, standing or sitting about the room, they began to help themselves to food. But their strained silence and sullen looks showed what they were feeling. As they were eating, Jesus began to talk to them about true greatness. Gently but firmly He pointed out that they must not be influenced by the pagan ideas of the world around them. He reminded them of what He had said only a few days earlier, when they were on the other side of the Jordan:

> The Kings of the Nations rule over them.
> Their tyrants take the title of 'Benefactor'.
> But you must not act on these lines . . .
> Let the greatest among you be as the younger,
> Let the leader be as one who serves.
> Which is the greatest, he who sits at the table or he who
>   waits on him?
> Is it not the guest?
> But I am among you as one who serves.

These quiet words fell like dew upon a sultry evening. Ashamed, and yet released, the young men stirred out of their uneasy silence. But still none of them could break through their embarrassment to serve the others. It was now time for the meal proper to begin. After a brief silence, in which no one moved, Jesus looked round at them all. Then without a word He bent down, picked up the basin, the towel and the jug of water by the door. Very quietly, kneeling before each one in turn, He washed their feet. And as He did so their anger and irritation faded away, leaving them quiet and wondering. 'Thy King cometh unto thee . . . meek', they had sung in triumph only a few days before; and now He was coming to *them*, to each one, in great humility, ' as One that serveth '.

The atmosphere was clearer when He rose from His knees. Peace breathed from Him. Not even the presence of Judas (during the earlier part of the evening), could break this strange peace which seemed to fill the quiet room, and made every man look kindly upon his brother. Presently Jesus broke the healing silence with cheering, encouraging words, which His bewildered friends greatly needed. Then He went on to speak gently, but surely, of ' betrayal ' and ' death ', and a cloud of sorrow and bewilderment enveloped them. What was He saying? Something about a ' last will and testament '?

And while they were wondering what He meant, during Supper Jesus took bread, gave thanks, and broke it, giving it to each one with the words: ' Take, eat, this is My Body which is broken for you.'[2] Then He took of the wine upon the Table, poured it into the Cup, and gave to each one, saying: ' This is my blood of the covenant, which is shed for many.'[3] Obediently, as in a dream, His friends received the bread and the wine at His hands. And as they looked into His face they saw such love that they knew—without words—that He was giving Himself to them—for ever.

Afterwards, He spoke to them in words they could never forget. Deeply imprinted upon their hearts, too, was the remembrance of His face as they sang together before they left the Upper Room: ' Return unto thy rest, O my soul, for the Lord hath dealt bountifully with thee. For thou hast delivered my soul from death, mine eyes from tears, and my feet from falling. I will walk before the Lord in the land of the living.'[4] And as He sang He looked up to heaven, and such a brightness shone in His face that for the moment they were reassured. But when He joined in the final Psalm and came to the words ' God is the Lord which hath shewed us light; bind the sacrifice with cords, even unto the horns of the altar. Thou art my God, and I will praise thee! Thou art my God and I will exalt thee! '[5] their voices faltered. They looked at Him in amazement: He seemed so full of joy that the only word to describe the expression on His face was—' glory '.

Suddenly, there was a knock on the door. A man entered, went up to Jesus and whispered something in His ear. Jesus

[2] I Cor. 11.24 (R.V. marg.)   [3] Mark 14.24 (R.V.).
[4] Ps. 116.7-9.   [5] Ps. 118.27-28.

nodded, turned to His friends and said: 'The hour has come. We must go.' So from the light and peace of the Upper Room the little company went out again into the dark streets. The moon had risen, and the path leading down into the Valley of the Kidron, and then up the rocky hill-side to the Olive Orchard of Gethsemane, was as bright as day. So they went into the Garden. Jesus withdrew into the deep shadow of the ancient olive trees . . . and prayed. For this was 'the same night that he was betrayed'.

CHAPTER I

THE SIGNIFICANCE OF THE SACRAMENT

ON that night 'in which he was betrayed',[1] Judas, the traitor, went out of the lighted room: 'and it was night'. Yet at that dark and tragic moment a fire was lit which has been burning ever since. For on that dark night Christ pledged Himself to us—for ever.

> *The eternal Fount is hidden in Living Bread,*
> *That we with Life eternal may be fed,*
> *Although 'tis night.*[2]

From that Upper Room there stretches an unbroken chain of light—like a chain of fires burning in the darkness—down the centuries to our own day. For the Eucharist is the central act of Christian worship. Wherever the Church takes root, there its life is quickened, nourished, and manifested in the celebration of the Sacrament. Just as the first thing we do in a new house is to light a fire, and the fire warms and hallows the new home, so wherever men have gone in their wanderings, the Sacrament has gone with them. For Christ is our home throughout the journey of life: 'He that is near Me is near the Fire.'

The Eucharist is central: because it gathers up, expresses, and makes effective the whole meaning of the spiritual life. It proclaims the Christian Gospel: in it God comes to us with His forgiveness and His strength. One by one, and as members of the Body of Christ, we respond to Him with gratitude and awe.

The meaning of the Eucharist is inexhaustible; it transcends all our efforts to explain or interpret it. We never come to the end of it. Long experience only deepens our wonder and our awe. In every age, in every part of the Church Universal, both in corporate worship and in the experience of the individual,

[1] I Cor. 11.23.   [2] *Poems*, St. John of the Cross.

glimpses are sometimes granted of the glory which lies behind
the Sacrament: one part of the Church will see one aspect, and
another will see something else, but the truth, the glory and the
depth of the Eucharist are beyond us all.

Here are two testimonies, coming from very different traditions.

'The Holy Eucharist is the . . . sacrament of Sacraments. It
is the richest, the most appealing, the most mysterious, the
tenderest of all. It gathers into its fathomless depths the un-
searchable riches of Christ.[3]

'In the Sacrament of the Lord's Supper many strains of
religious belief and experience come together. Indeed, in this
Sacrament the whole of what our religion means is expressed.
That which otherwise we apprehend piecemeal is integrated in
a rite which presents it all as the sheer gift of God. On any one
occasion we may be conscious only of this or that element in the
meaning; but it is all there, because God in Christ is there. In
dependence on Him for everything we render it all back to Him
in thankful adoration.'[4]

It is indeed amazing to see the richness and variety of the
experience which has grown out of those few quiet words and
that simple ceremony at the Supper on 'the night in which he
was betrayed'. From age to age this experience is not only
repeated, it is deepened and enlarged. God alone could have
created this wealth of experience and meaning. Yet with all
this wide variety, the Sacrament itself is something very
strong, simple and abiding. Through all the changes of life
it stands there, like a great Rock, unchanging amidst all the
changes of light and shade, night and day, fair weather and
storm.

Something of this vast significance comes out in the fact that
no one name for the rite ever expresses the whole: 'Holy Communion' denotes one element, but excludes others; the 'Lord's
Supper' and 'Breaking of Bread' express the historic basis and
the fellowship or 'community' character of the Sacrament. The
words 'Eucharist' and 'Oblation', which come from the very
early days of the life of the Church, stress the essential elements
of 'worship' and 'offering'. 'The Holy Sacrifice'—a title much
used by some of the Early Fathers—emphasizes the sacrificial
aspect.

[3] Leen, By Jacob's Well.
[4] Christian Worship, ed. by N. Micklem, p. 82 (C. H. Dodd).

Thus it is evident that no doctrine of the Eucharist which lays all the emphasis upon *one* aspect alone can possibly explain why the Eucharist is the central act of the Church's worship. It is only when all these different elements or aspects are seen to be part of a single act of worship which includes, unites and transcends them all, that something of the wonder of the Eucharist begins to dawn upon us. For the Eucharist, as God's gift to us, is as deep as His action, and goes far beyond all human ' vision ', feeling, consciousness or thought.

II

The Eucharist is a personal encounter. It is the place where God and man meet—within the life of the Church. Sometimes the Lord's Supper is described as a ' symbol '. If by this we mean a mere ' picture ' or ' metaphor ' then our view is still imperfect and superficial. For the deep and ancient meaning of a ' symbol ' is a ' coming-together ', a ' meeting ', or an ' encounter '. Only in this sense is the Eucharist ' symbolical '. All that we find here points to, and opens the way into the heart of Reality. Here, in this act and in this rite—God comes to man—the sinner meets his Saviour.

In the words of a German Lutheran writer of the seventeenth century: ' Just as the sun shines most brightly at midday, so the love of the Son of God shines most gloriously in this wonderful Supper. Here He has opened His divine heart wide to us, like a rose in full bloom. He does not give me His garment or His picture, nor silver nor gold . . . but Himself. When I approach Him I see Him, in spirit, wounded for our sakes, and I hear Him say: ' Come unto Me, all of you . . .' When I leave the table my soul saith: ' My Friend is mine and I am His.'[5]

In this chapter, it is true, we are thinking of the Eucharist as the act of the Church, as the central action of the whole Christian community, and we cannot insist on this truth too often or too strongly. How much we lose, and how much the Church loses, when its members treat the Sacrament of the whole People of God—of the whole Christian family—as a private and even an individualistic affair! But although this kind of ' individualism ' and ' private-mindedness ' is contrary to the very spirit of the

[5] *Christian Scriver* (d. 1693). *Die Geschichte der Abendmahlsfrömmigkeit in Zeugnissen und Berichten*, by Hans Preuss, p. 12.

Sacrament, it is also true that there is no act in which we become more fully personal than at the Lord's Table.

A man may come to the Sacrament feeling that he counts for very little in the eyes of other people. He may be lonely, through no fault of his own. He may have had peculiar difficulties, which have isolated him, to some extent, from his fellows, and have sapped his self-confidence. He may be neither 'clever' nor 'outstanding'. He does his duty as well as he can, but no one takes much notice of him; his work and his service are taken for granted, in the Church as well as in daily life. But when he comes to the Lord's Table he is not treated like this. He is *welcomed*, with an inexpressible personal love. For he realizes— more perhaps than the people who are 'successful' and popular —that the Eucharist is the expression of God's desire to draw near to His children.

For in the Eucharist we find that God wants us much more than we want Him. And He wants us because He loves us. So when we 'draw near' in this act of worship we can be more than sure that we are welcomed, forgiven, and restored, because we are 'endlessly loved'. As Christ draws near to each one of us, the most discouraged finds new hope. For to each of us He says: 'I have loved *thee* with an everlasting love: therefore with loving-kindness have I drawn thee.'[6] So the most isolated, troubled, tempted person finds in this Sacrament love and understanding, forgiveness and strength, and courage to face life. For Christ makes him a 'person'—someone who 'counts'.

III

The Eucharist is *effective*: it *does* something, as P. T. Forsyth is never tired of saying. At the Last Supper, Jesus *did* something. Under the shadow of His imminent death, He *acted*: looking forward to the next few hours—the climax of His life of self-giving to God and man, He says (in effect) to His friends at the table: 'All I have been doing, all I am, is *yours*. . . . I am about to seal this offering with My death.'

This Sacrament is not an 'object-lesson'—something to stir our feelings for a moment and then to be swiftly forgotten in the next trivial experience that claims our attention. Nor is it the reiteration of a timeless truth, which we have to 'realize' or

[6] Jer. 31.3.

'remember' or 'try to understand'. We do not come to the Sacrament to learn something with our minds: we come to meet God. This rite of worship is a creative act. God and man meet, and something happens. This creative power of the Eucharist is clearly God's creative act of redemption, offered to us anew in every celebration of the Sacrament. For its inexhaustible significance springs from the fact that the Eucharist 'is the precious vehicle of God's loving purpose to save lost mankind'.

Thus the fundamental value of the Sacrament lies in the act of God: in the fact that *God* has done all, before we knew anything about it; it does not depend upon *our* faith; indeed, it is this act of God which creates and evokes faith. The Sacrament is based upon something which God has *done*—once for all. Forsyth never tires of insisting on this truth that the Sacrament is the work of *God*: based on the act of God in Christ reconciling Himself to the world on the Cross; it is this act which creates the Sacrament, and gives it its inexhaustible meaning and power, though 'the vast part of its range is beyond our conscious grasp of experience'.[7]

In some sections of the Christian Church there is a widespread impression—amounting sometimes to a positive conviction—that all 'experience' in the Christian life must be equated with 'feeling'—in the sense of emotion or of 'intensified awareness'. This heresy (if I may so describe it) works havoc in the spiritual life, both of the individual and of the community. If it is unchecked, it leads to a habit of morbid introspection, breeds unhealthy scruples, and may in extreme cases lead to the loss of all real faith in God and interest in other people. There is no finer corrective for such an attitude than this objective view of the Sacrament as *God's Act*—quite apart from anything we can do or feel. In the Eucharist God *acts*—we receive and adore. Opening our hearts to Christ, submitting to His action, we receive fresh grace and strength from Himself, apart from any 'feeling' we may or may not have, at the time of communicating. For in this rite, as a whole, He gives us all we need—in Himself.

IV

Even where the significance of the Sacrament is largely hidden from the worshipper, either owing to faulty teaching, or to lack of teaching, or to his own ignorance, or to carelessness and blind-

[7] P. T. Forsyth, *The Church and the Sacraments*, p. 217.

ness, due to sin or lack of discipline in daily life, no one can fail
to be aware of the awe, the silence, and the gravity which sur-
rounds every reverent celebration of the Sacrament, whether this
takes place with the utmost simplicity, in some bare hall or upper
room, or in a church or cathedral with all the splendour of the
Liturgy.

A young child was once sent up into the gallery of a large
(non-Anglican) church while the Sacrament of the Lord's Supper
was being celebrated below. She was too far away to hear any
words; but the sight of the congregation, absorbed in this act of
worship—of her parents, lost in some reality greater than themselves—the slow reverent movements of the officiating minister,
and of the elders as they moved quietly from pew to pew, the
whiteness of the 'fair linen cloth' on the Communion Table,
and—above all—the silence, made a lasting impression on her
young mind. Dimly, and perhaps hardly consciously, she was
already aware that God was here, acting and living, in this 'brief,
grave and still Sacrament'.

The quality of this silence at the Lord's Table is like no other
silence: it is a living stillness, palpitating with life. Even the
most careless worshipper is awed—for a time. For this silence
has something of the 'homeliness of Eternity'. Those who do
not know 'what it's all about' may perhaps be bored, and wish
that 'the service were over'; but for those who come with prepared hearts and minds the silence can never be too long. For in
this silence they know that they are overshadowed by the wings
of the Divine Mercy, gathering all under His shelter. Beyond
words, beyond feeling—they know: 'Jesus is near . . . all is
well'.

For here, all that matters is *God*: what He is, what He has
done, what He is doing *now*, and what He will do 'at the end'
when God will be 'all in all'. Here God gives and we receive.
He acts, and we adore. He is, and we depend utterly upon him.
The Eucharist begins with God: 'Prayer,' says Dr. Forsyth, 'is
a gift and sacrifice that *we* make; sacrament is a gift and sacrifice
that God makes. . . . In prayer we go to God, in Sacrament
He comes to us.'[8]

Friedrich von Hügel, in a famous passage, speaking of the
ardent devotion of St. Catherine of Genoa to the Holy Eucharist,
says:

'She found here the Infinite first condescending to the finite,

[8] P. T. Forsyth, *The Church and the Sacraments*, pp. 224-225.

so that the finite may rise towards the Infinite; . . . God, giving
Himself through such apparently slight vehicles, in such short
moments, and under such bewilderingly humble veils.'[9]   The
Eucharist begins with God; it is an act of God; it ends in God:
'All goes out in mystery'.   For the Eucharist unites earth and
heaven.   At every celebration, time, as we know it, fades away,
and through Christ we are united with the Church Triumphant.
As we worship, saying, 'Holy, Holy, Holy,' we join with saints
and angels, and with the spirits of just men made perfect, and
with the great assembly of the first-born now in heaven.   Time
and space do not matter; here we touch Eternity.

v

From the general significance of the Sacrament we now turn to
the particular.   In our actual experience, in our life in the
Church, and in our personal life of faith, what does the Eucharist
mean?   Which aspect predominates?   Worship and self-offering?
or communion with Christ?   or the 'memorial' and historical
element?   or the Sacrament as a source of energy?   or as an act of
fellowship?

Most of us would agree that every one of these aspects is
essential to the full meaning of this Sacrament.   Yet we shall
certainly understand this rite better, and take part in it with
greater freedom, if we look at each element separately, and consider each in turn.   We cannot afford to ignore any of these
elements, though probably one aspect or another may predominate
at different periods in our lives.

The essential elements in the liturgy of the Eucharist have been
analysed by various writers, notably by Evelyn Underhill and by
Bishop Brilioth (of the Lutheran Church of Sweden).[10]   Here I
follow the analysis given by Evelyn Underhill in her book on
Worship.[11]   She suggests that these different aspects, as represented in the great Eastern and Western Liturgies, are six:

1. *Adoration and Thanksgiving*: the 'setting' of the whole
   act of worship, which from the outset is turned towards
   God Transcendent.
2. *The Memorial of the Passion*: the historical element—God
   Incarnate in His saving action.

9 Friedrich von Hügel, *The Mystical Element of Religion*, Vol. I, p. 241.
10 Brilioth, *Eucharistic Faith and Practice*.   11 E. Underhill, *Worship*, p. 139.

3. *The Sacrificial Centre* : 'the heart of the action'; the offering of Christ and of the worshippers.
4. *The Royal Priesthood* : the supplications of the Church, made in union with this 'prevailing sacrifice'.
5. *The Heavenly Food* : eternal life.
6. *The Mystery of the Presence* : communion.

Thus the individual worshipper who yields himself fully to the action of the Eucharist will find that he is caught up into a creative movement which carries him far beyond himself. Drawn by 'the Love which moves the sun and all the other stars' he becomes part of the great rhythm of 'giving and receiving' which unites God and man. For first of all he adds his small offering of praise to the great Hymn of Praise which arises to God from the whole Creation. Then he responds to God's sacrificial love by offering his whole life, body and soul, as a living sacrifice, which is his 'reasonable service', and in this act of self-offering he finds his own life blessed and transformed. Finally, when he has offered his worship and his whole life to God, he enters into the sacred experience of communion, where he is fed with heavenly food and is received by the Lord Himself. And all this rich and ever-expanding experience comes to him not as a solitary individual, intent on his own 'perfection' or 'consolation', but as a member of the Body of Christ as a whole. Here, as part of the Body, he offers himself to God that he may share in the apostolic and priestly work of bringing the whole world back to God.

PRAYERS

We give thanks to Thee, O Lord God, Father Almighty, together with Thy Son our Lord God and Saviour Jesus Christ, and the Holy Spirit, and we offer unto Thee this reasonable service, which all nations offer unto Thee, O Lord, from the rising of the sun unto the going down thereof, from the North and from the South: for great is Thy Name in all nations, and in every place incense and sacrifice and oblation are offered unto Thy Holy Name.

LITURGY OF ST. MARK

O taste and see how good the Lord is, Alleluia! Bless the Lord in the heavens, Alleluia! Bless Him in the highest, Alleluia! Bless

Him, all ye angels of His, Alleluia! Bless Him, all His host, Alleluia!
What blessing or thanksgiving can we offer for this Sacrament?
Thee only, O Jesus, do we bless, with the Father and the most Holy
Spirit, now and for ever. Amen.

ARMENIAN LITURGY

What blessing, or what praise, or what thanksgiving, can we render
to Thee, O God, the Lover of men, for that when we were cast away
by the doom of death, and drowned in the depth of sin, Thou hast
granted us freedom, and bestowed on us this immortal and heavenly
Food, and manifested to us this Mystery hid from ages and from
generations? Grant us to understand this Thy supreme act of mercy,
and the greatness of Thy Fatherly care for us.

COPTIC LITURGY OF ST. CYRIL

CHAPTER II

WORSHIP AND THE EUCHARIST

Genuine Christian worship, whatever its special emphasis may be, always requires as its foundation belief in One Holy and Eternal God, the Being of Beings, the Maker, Lover, and Keeper of all life; utterly transcendent to His Creation, and yet fully present with and in it; besetting, sustaining, moulding, above all, loving all that is made. . . . The greatest passages in the New Testament and the earliest of our liturgical documents alike witness decisively to this profoundly theocentric character of primitive Christian worship; its awed sense of the vast divine Action, its Apocalyptic insistence on the eternal significance of Jesus, the Lamb ' slain from the foundation of the world ', its constant otherworldly reference to ' the deep things of God '.

EVELYN UNDERHILL

We are nothing in ourselves but darkness, yet in Holy Communion, having received Christ who is the Father's Glory, we now have true glory to give to the Father. . . . Our worship at the Altar is our recognition of the Word made flesh, and our grateful love coming forth clothed in the sunshine of His Presence, to welcome and carry His glory in the highest . . . in our praise and thanksgiving. . . . Every ' Gloria' brings us back to our fellowship with angels and archangels, and rekindles the light of the Gospel of the Glory of God in our praise. And this sacrifice of praise and thanksgiving that springs in the morning Eucharist is given to us to be a light that is to go on shining—a river of light that is to run through every day, in praise. . . . For we are called to glorify God in all that we are doing for Him, and that is a glory for eternity. . . . The glory of Christ will be a transforming energy in us.

FR. CONGREVE

THE Eucharist is the central act of Christian worship. This is not a theory. It is a fact. From the very beginning of the Christian Church the Eucharist has been the universal expression of Christian corporate worship; the worship of the Body of Christ as a whole. It was already at the heart of Christian life and faith twenty years before the first documents of the New Testament were written. For more than a hundred years apostles, martyrs and unknown saints, as well as countless 'ordinary' men and women, were strengthened, and enabled to live and work and suffer for Christ before the New Testament, as we know it, had become the standard 'scripture', in addition to the Old Testament. Thus Eucharistic worship was not based on the Bible but on tradition, that is, on practice.

We have only to look at the New Testament to see how rich in meaning the Eucharist already was in the life of the Church, which began with the 'single rite of the broken Bread and the blessed Cup'. It is the solemn proclamation of the Lord's death; it is also the joyful manifestation of His Living Presence as the Risen Lord. It gathers up the whole meaning of sacrifice, and looks forward to the glorious future when 'God will be all in all', and all things will be gathered up and restored in Christ. These are only a few of the allusions to that act of worship which already existed in the Primitive Church, as a complete summary of 'the Gospel' before the Four Gospels were written.

There was of course a great variety of expression, but behind and underneath it all the basic structure of the rite was the same. It was due to the laity that the rigid outline of the rite was preserved; and this was due to the fact that the Eucharist as a whole was the corporate act of the whole Church. In those early days, when the Church was young, and much that we now possess was in a very fluid condition, it was this practice of Eucharistic worship, expressed in a liturgy, which unified the Church, and was the living channel through which its life was transmitted from one generation to another. This unity was not imposed from without; it sprang from within, from the heart of worship itself, from the act of a whole body of Christians in a certain place offering to God together their adoring praise. For 'in the Eucharist the unity of the Body expresses itself in united acts of praise and adoration, bursting forth into such exalted moments as those of the *Sursum Corda*, the *Sanctus*, and the *Gloria*. It is not living on and expressing the splendid reality of its own communal life, but its entire indebtedness to God for accepting it in the Beloved '.[1] The worship of the Eucharist is central because in it the Church makes her adoring response to the total revelation of God in Christ.

This is why the service begins with the revealed Word. That is: the first note struck in this rite is not the need of the worshippers, but the fact of revelation. From the very first the Christian Church realized that all worship must begin with God Transcendent. It is from such a God that we receive the revelation of His Being and His purpose. We begin with God, the high and Holy One, ' who inhabiteth eternity '. We listen, first of all, to His Word.

Preaching is a vital part of worship, and at the Eucharist its function is to bring home to the worshippers the reality of all that God has done for us in Christ; it is only as we realize what we owe to God that we are drawn to worship Him. The readings from Scripture, the Epistle and Gospel, are also part of this Ministry of the Word. Both the readings and the sermon are intended to be part of the direct preparation of the worshippers for the Eucharist itself. To this proclamation of the Gospel we respond with prayer and praise.

II

It is, however, only too easy to attend Church regularly, and even to ' go to Communion ', and yet to miss the point of it all. There may be different reasons for this, but whatever the cause may be, our ability to worship with any sense of freedom will be seriously hampered. Some people who are in this state feel dimly that ' there must be a clue '. Others do not realize that there is one at all. They simply go to Church from habit and a sense of duty; they do not even think there is anything further to be expected.

If we are conscious of a sense of dulness or unreality in worship, there is one cause which is our own fault. We all have an inveterate tendency to think about everything in terms which affect *ourselves*: for instance, we hear that someone we know is ill and cannot keep an engagement; usually our instinctive reaction is not: ' What can I do to help? ' but ' How very tiresome! ' This tendency often creeps into our religious practices, and this fatal drift towards self-occupation spoils our efforts to

[1] J. K. Mozley, *The Gospel Sacraments*, p. 110.

worship God. The very fact that people will sometimes say to us when we come back from Church: 'Did you have a good service?' or 'Did you enjoy it?' encourages this habit of mind. It is only too easy to respond in kind, and to begin to complain of the preacher, or of the way in which the service was 'read' or conducted, or to say 'the choir was shockingly bad this morning', or 'I don't know *why* So-and-so is *allowed* to play the organ!' All these remarks may be perfectly correct, and justified as statements of facts; but so far as worship is concerned they are beside the mark. It is true that any of these defects may make worship more difficult, but to those who sincerely want to worship God, they will not be insuperable.

So before we consider Eucharistic worship we may well remind ourselves first of all of the nature of worship in general.

Worship is a universal practice. The prayer-flags of Tibet, the great temples of Hinduism, the mosques of Islam, and the spirit-huts in the great African forests, all bear witness to the fact that all over the world men and women are reaching out to a Being greater than themselves, a Being or a Spirit, to whom they feel they must *offer* something—or someone—often at great cost to themselves. In whatever form this worship may be offered, and however far it may be from the truth of the Christian revelation, it is always a response to an objective reality, a reality which either fascinates or repels the worshipper, filling him either with longing or with fear and awe. Thus when we try to worship as Christians, we are not doing something as an 'extra'; it is an instinctive practice, carried on all over the world, which has been a marked feature of man's life from the very earliest days. In the words of Evelyn Underhill, worship extends from 'the puzzled upward glance of the primitive to the delighted self-oblation of the saint'.[2]

Thus it is the function of the Church of Christ to be *the* worshipping community—the one body in which the vague or mistaken longings of mankind are gathered up, transformed, and expressed in true worship. The Church is bound to put worship first in her life; everything else springs from it. For the central act of religion is humble adoration. In the last resort, nothing matters but *God*. He alone *is*. All our life—seen and unseen, past, present, and future—depends upon Him. Were He to withdraw His hand for a moment from the universe the whole structure would dissolve, like the 'baseless fabric of a

[2] *Worship*, p. 4.

dream'. He sustains and upholds all things by the word of His power.

The deepest reason for worship, however, does not lie in this sense of need and dependence—true though this is—it lies rather in the awed and adoring recognition of the fact that God has supreme rights over us. By His acts in creation and redemption we belong to Him, whether we are aware of this or not. In true worship we gladly accept this fact, and yield ourselves to Him in obedience. Above all, in worship we rejoice in God's perfection; we are thankful that God is God, infinite in glory, love, and power. To look away from ourselves to God brings a great sense of expansion and liberation; we forget ourselves in wondering at God; and the height of worship is reached in the adoring hymn:

> Holy! Holy! Holy! Lord God of Hosts! Heaven and earth are full of Thy glory! Glory be to Thee, O Lord Most High . . . We give Thee thanks for Thy great glory.

III

The earliest reflection of Eucharistic worship is found in the New Testament itself. The vision of the Living Lord[3] which came to the exiled 'witness' in the little island in the Ægean Sea was evidently connected with the experience of joining 'in spirit' with the worship of his own church at home, in the celebration of the Eucharist. Again, the message to the Church at Laodicea suggests the need for penitence and the readiness of Christ to come to the individual soul in the Blessed Supper: 'Behold! I stand at the door and knock: if any man hear my voice, and open the door, I will come in to him, and will sup with him, and he with me.'[4] In this same book of *Revelation* the numerous descriptions of worship 'in heaven' are obviously based on the worship on earth, as the writer and the readers knew it. The inspired writer—in his pictorial language—suggests the reality and power of the worship offered by the Church on earth. Worship is here presented as man's adoring response to God, praising Him for all that He is and for all that He has done.

Evelyn Underhill suggests that 'eucharistic action' runs right through the New Testament: that it is suggested in the Feeding of the Five Thousand, in the opening phrases of the Lord's

[3] Rev. 1.12ff.　　　[4] Rev. 3.20.

Prayer, as well as in many other parts of the Gospels and Epistles, as well as in the book of Revelation. The key-note of Eucharistic worship—which sets the pattern for all the great Eucharistic prayers of the Early Church—is sounded in this ascription of praise in the book of Revelation: 'Worthy art thou, our Lord and our God, to receive the glory and the honour and the power: for thou didst create all things, and because of thy will they were, and were created.'[5]

Indeed the very word Eucharist (or Thanksgiving) means this whole-hearted adoring thankfulness to God, and delight in God, a heartfelt and willing surrender to Him, which is characteristic of worship in the New Testament.

The earliest records of the life of the Primitive Church are full of this spirit of thanksgiving and adoration. In an early manual of Christian life and church order, the *Didache*, the instruction for the administration of the Eucharist is couched in the following terms:

'First, as to the Cup, we give thanks to Thee Our Father, for the Holy Vine of David, Thy servant, which Thou didst make known to us through Jesus Thy servant. . . . Then, as to the broken bread: we give thanks to Thee, our Father, for the life and knowledge which Thou didst make known to us through Jesus, Thy servant. . . . Glory be to Thee for ever.'

Further on there is another prayer of thanksgiving:

'We thank Thee, Holy Father, for Thy Holy Name, which Thou hast made to dwell in our hearts, and for the knowledge, faith and immortality which Thou didst make known to us through Jesus Thy Servant. Glory be to Thee for ever. Thou, Almighty Lord, didst create all things for Thy Name's sake, and gavest food and drink for men to enjoy, that they might give thanks unto Thee; and to us didst vouchsafe spiritual food and drink . . . and life eternal through Thy Servant. Above all, we thank Thee because Thou art mighty. Glory be to Thee for ever.'[6]

Another early description of the celebration of the Eucharist comes to us from the second century, from Justin Martyr (*c.* A.D. 150); here, too, there is the emphasis upon thanksgiving, closely connected with the thanksgiving offered by our Lord at the Last Supper:[7]

'Jesus took bread, and gave thanks, and said: This do in

[5] Rev. 4.11 (R.V.).   [6] J. H. Srawley, *The Early History of the Liturgy*, pp. 18ff.
[7] Ibid., pp. 30ff.

remembrance of Me; this is My Body; and He likewise took the Cup, and after He had given thanks, said, this is My Blood.'

The early liturgies are full of this spirit of grateful adoration. The main theme of these great prayers is thanksgiving for God's great acts in creation, for 'the glory that fills heaven and earth'; and then for the supreme act of His creative and redeeming love in the coming of Christ to earth 'in the form of a servant', for His incarnation, and His continued self-giving to the needs of men. These Eucharistic prayers are splendidly objective; they are concerned with God and His glory, not with the subjective feelings and needs of the worshippers. They breathe the atmosphere of eternity, and lift us up to God.

' Lift up your hearts!' cries the priest, and the people respond: ' We lift them up unto the Lord.' The *Sursum Corda* is followed by a prayer of this kind:

' It is verily meet and right, holy and becoming . . . Lord God, Father Almighty, to worship Thee, to hymn Thee, to give thanks unto Thee, to return Thee praise both night and day, with unceasing mouth, and lips that keep not silence, and hearts that cannot be still.'[8]

In these early liturgies, the note of joy and praise predominates, for the Church on earth is praising God with the Church in heaven; and every act of worship contains at its heart this supreme act of adoration—though the expression may differ slightly in the various prayers:

' Holy! Holy! Holy! Lord God of Sabaoth! Heaven and earth are full of Thy holy Glory! Hosanna in the Highest! Blessed is He that cometh in the Name of the Lord: Hosanna in the Highest!'

As we try to enter into this worship of the Church down the ages we almost feel as though we were joining hands and taking part in a sacred dance. For God calls all His children to play His game. In Eucharistic worship we are moving together, hand in hand, in time, and in tune, with the glorious will of God, with our faces to the Light, as we move according to the rhythm of love: love to God and love to man. For our praises are offered unceasingly to the 'Love that moves the sun and the other stars'.

IV

Most of us, however, if we are quite honest, would admit that
[8] *Liturgy of St. Mark.*

this adoring thankfulness and worship does not come easily to us. We are not only 'bound by the chain of our sins' but by our 'distractions'—by all that fills our minds and hearts apart from God—thoughts which float through our minds without any apparent reference to God at all. Nowhere do these 'distractions' become so 'distracting' as when we are making a sincere effort to worship God, and to forget ourselves. Of course there may be a good many reasons for this mood of 'distraction'; it may be due to ill-health, over-fatigue, and overwork; to pressing anxieties for others, or to the necessities of making a living. When this is the case, we can be very sure that God understands and cares, and that He is not 'down' on us for such pre-occupations—all that He asks from us is that we should come to Him *as we are*, and give ourselves, and those we love, and the world in its need, into His Hands.

There is, however, a far more real cause for distraction, namely, inattention to God. If we pay little or no attention to God throughout the week we shall naturally find it difficult, and even impossible, to throw ourselves heart and soul into the central act of worship of the Church on Sunday. If our prayers are brief and perfunctory; if we meditate on the truths of the Christian faith rarely or spasmodically, or perhaps not at all; if we are more concerned with our own affairs, our duties and pleasures and interests than with God—it stands to reason that it will be very difficult to worship truly when we do go to Church, and still more, at the Eucharist.

We know that we are not saints, and that often their expressions of delight in worship leave us cold. It is no use running away from the truth about ourselves by saying, 'After all, I am made that way! I am not spiritual.' We were *made* for God, and if we do not bring Him the worship and love that He desires, we are grieving and disobeying Him, and losing our own souls into the bargain. Indeed, we are missing the whole meaning of life, both for ourselves, and for the service we might render to our fellows.

We must begin where we are. This means that we must come to the Sacrament as *sinners*. There is no need to wait to 'feel' this. We must accept the fact that this disinclination for worship, this boredom with spiritual things, these excuses for evading the claims of God, are simply a form of 'escapism'. We are sinners: and we miss the whole point of the Sacrament unless we accept this as a fact. People often say that they cannot or dare not communicate because they are not 'worthy'. A story is told of an old Presbyterian scholar who was often afflicted with doubts about his 'worthiness' to receive the Sacrament. One day when he was sitting in his pew, waiting for the officiating elder to bring the elements, he noticed a young girl near him weeping bitterly, and he saw that she hesitated to take the Bread when it was offered to her. Instantly he forgot himself and his own scruples, leant forward and said to her in an urgent undertone: 'Take it! Take it! It's for *sinners*!'

Péguy said once: 'The sinner is at the very heart of Christendom.' By this he means that the sinner who knows he is a sinner, and is sorry and repentant, knows 'what Christianity is about, because to him sin and grace, mercy and forgiveness are not words learnt in a catechism, but realities known in the immediacy of bitter experience'. It is as forgiven, grateful sinners that we come again and again to the Lord's Table, to be forgiven and renewed, and to be given new strength for the fight against sin. From such hearts there will rise continually a constant stream of thanksgiving and worship.

But the Eucharistic worship means more than this. The sense of our sinfulness, which increases with years and experience, makes us realize that no one can possibly offer 'worthy' worship. We know that we are wholly unable to give God the worship which His infinite worth requires. 'Even the most devoted human being who has ever lived, even the whole human race from the beginning to the end of time, even the angelic hosts of heaven, cannot render to God that infinite honour to which His perfection entitles Him. So we find, in all or almost all the races of mankind, a profound consciousness that we can make a worthy offering to God only if, before we offer it to Him, He has taken it and transformed it into something which is good enough for Him. 'This,' says Dr. Mascall, 'is at least one of the roots of the universal institution of *sacrifice*, in which, under a bewildering variety of forms, men offer to God different kinds of gifts which are consecrated to this use by some priestly ritual act.'[9]

The history of religions shows very clearly that no human act of worship is ever adequate; each offering only bears witness to the sense of need and desire, but it does not carry with it any sense of fulfilment. For God alone can offer perfect worship. Christ alone, as the God-Man, has made the one perfect, unspoilt

[9] E. L. Mascall, *Christ, the Christian, and the Church*, p. 160.

offering to God. By His Life of unbroken obedience to the Father's Will, for the first time on earth, man offered an act of worship which was adequate and complete, so as the end of His earthly life drew near, He was able to say, 'I have glorified thee on the earth; I have finished the work which thou gavest me to do.'[10]

Thus it is through Him, through Christ, and through Him alone, that we can offer acceptable worship to God at the Eucharist. Here Christ takes our imperfect worship, our stumbling prayers, our weak and fitful desires as well as our deepest and best longings, and unites them with His own worship in the heavenly places. Thus through Him we are able to worship the Father 'in spirit and in truth'.

We cannot remind ourselves too often that this priority of worship in the Eucharist is the keynote of the whole of the Christian life: namely, that the life of prayer and worship does not aim first of all at the comforting or the perfecting of the individual soul—as we often think it does and should. The aim of all worship, and of the Eucharist in particular, is the transformation of the whole of life: bringing everything under the rule of God; offering all we have and are to the purposes of God. This is the end for which we have been made. Thus our worship at the Eucharist is both an offering to God, and a token of the offering of our life to the doing of His Will.

To worship thus will also have a great influence upon our relations with other people. Unless in some measure it does this for us, we may well wonder whether we have entered into worship at all. It will also transfigure our attitude to our duties, especially those which often seem tiresome and insignificant: the daily things that 'have to be done', whether we like it or not. All this rather arid side of life can be transformed, and used, as we offer it to God for His purposes, in cheerful obedience. Again, the Eucharist will give an added radiance to all beauty, and to all our holidays and recreations. If this kind of worship is at the heart of our lives, we shall find increasingly that the whole of life, sorrow as well as joy, suffering as well as work, ordinary duties and special emergencies, will be unified and transfigured by God's gracious acceptance of our will to serve and praise Him in everything. For every time we receive Christ in the Eucharist, we receive the power to bring something of His beauty and tenderness and strength into every part of our lives. When we

[10] John 17.4.

worship in this way we can echo the prayer of St. Chrysostom
(his last words): 'Glory be to God for all things.'

DIVINE PRAISES
(St. Francis of Assisi)

Most Powerful, Most Holy, Most High and Sovereign God,
Thou art all Good, and the only Good:
To Thee do we render all praise, all honour, and all blessing.
Thou art the Lord God, who alone workest wonders. . . .
Thou art the Holy Father, King of Heaven and earth. . . .
Thou art Beauty. . . .
Thou art our great Sweetness. . . .
Great and wonderful is my Lord God Almighty,
Bountiful and Merciful Saviour.

Our mouths are filled with joy and our tongues with exultation,
because we are made partakers, O Lord, of Thine Immortal Sacra-
ment; because the things which eye hath not seen, nor ear heard,
neither hath it entered into the heart of man to conceive, Thou hast
revealed to those that love Thy Name, and to the little ones of Thy
Holy Church. . . . Even so, Father, for so it seemed good in Thy
sight: for Thou art merciful; and to Thee we ascribe glory, honour
and adoration, Father, Son and Holy Ghost, now and for ever and to
all ages. Amen.

COPTIC LITURGY OF ST. BASIL

O all ye works of the Lord, bless the Lord: praise and exalt Him
above all for ever.

O ye Angels of the Lord, bless the Lord: bless the Lord, O ye
heavens.

Let us bless the Father, and the Son with the Holy Ghost: let us
praise and exalt Him above all for ever.

Blessed art Thou, O Lord, in the Firmament of Heaven: and
worthy to be praised and glorified, and exalted above all for ever.

FROM THE BENEDICITE

CHAPTER III

'IN REMEMBRANCE OF ME'

. . . one of the soldiers with a spear pierced his side, and forthwith came there out blood and water.

JOHN 19.34

He caused His side to be thrown so widely open, and to be so deeply pierced, in order that the way that Thou mightest draw near to the heart of thy Beloved should be made plain to thee . . . draw near therefore to that Heart so exalted, but made so low for thee; to the Heart of God, who is so far above thee, but who opens to thee His door. . . . Do thou then take from the Saviour this Cup of love. Give thy heart to Him, who has opened His to thee.

THOMAS À KEMPIS

The Eucharist recalls the past, it is true, but it ever renews it, causing it to be actually present. Its commemoration is historical because it is a true remembrance of a past event in our Lord's history. But it does far more. It brings back the event which it recalls; it has power to make it an ever-living reality. . . . The same Presence is before us again and again, as real and true as when first vouchsafed ' in the same night that He was betrayed '.

T. T. CARTER

'THIS do, in remembrance of me.'[1] Every time we go to the Sacrament we hear these words. As we know, they come from the words of Institution in the First Epistle to the Corinthians. This means that they are very early; that the actual *words* would have been repeated so often by the first missionaries that they were

[1] I Cor. 11.24 and 25.

C

engraven, as it were, upon their minds and hearts, and it was these words that they passed on to the young Christian churches long before the Gospels were written.

Thus every time that we take part in the Eucharist, we are ourselves another link in the chain of uninterrupted celebration of the Sacrament, which has never ceased, from the Last Supper down to the present moment. We are in a glorious succession. Think of Polycarp, Bishop of Smyrna, who had learned much of Christ from John, the disciple of the Lord, at Ephesus, and was an intimate friend of 'those who had seen the Lord'. Born about the year 70 (or possibly a little earlier) Polycarp, as a young man, must have often worshipped at the Eucharist when John was officiating. How moving it must have been for him to hear the words: 'This do in remembrance of me', pronounced by one who had known the Lord on earth. It was in this faith and love that Polycarp lived and prayed and served Christ, and in this faith he died. He was a very old man when persecution broke out at Smyrna.[2] Yet when he was brought before the authorities and urged to sacrifice to Cæsar, and thus to save his life, he had only one thing to say: 'Eighty and six years have I served Christ, and He never did me wrong; how can I now blaspheme my King that has saved me?' When he was bound to the stake and about to be burned, he prayed: 'I bless Thee that Thou hast thought me worthy of the present day and hour, to have a share in the number of martyrs, and in the Cup of Christ, unto the resurrection of eternal life.'

Polycarp had kept the 'feast of Redemption' all through his long and blameless life. He had 'remembered' Christ in the Sacrament, but it was no mere 'memory' but His living Presence that strengthened him for service and endurance to the very end. Polycarp drank the 'Cup of Christ' when he gave his body to be burned rather than deny his Lord.

So when we come together to 'remember' Christ at the Eucharist this is no mere 'memorial'. Indeed the English words, 'remembrance' or 'memorial', do not render the real meaning of the Greek word *anamnesis*. They suggest something 'past' and 'absent', whereas *anamnesis* is rather a 'calling to mind' or a 're-calling'. When we 'call to mind' an event which means a great deal to us we think of it with all its associations; when we call a person to mind—especially if he or she is a person who means a great deal to us—we think of him or her with a kind of

[2] *c*. A.D. 155.

brooding concentration; we remind ourselves of their appearance, of the things they have said, of their actions, which have spoken louder than any words could do of the beauty and steadfastness of their character; we think of their relation to us, and we know that if we have real love and friendship we possess something imperishable, something which no separation can ever take away from us. We belong to each other.

Further, this 're-calling' means that something 'past' becomes 'present', something which, here and now, affects us vitally and profoundly. In other words, 'the Eucharist is the "memorial" —that is, the *anamnesis*, the making present—of the true Paschal Lamb who is the Christ. Indeed, the Church's sole warrant for celebrating the Eucharist at all is that in obedience to Christ's command, she is doing, as His representative and instrument, what He Himself did . . . "in the same night that He was betrayed"'.[3] In one of Kierkegaard's moving meditations at the service of Holy Communion he urges his hearers to remember that 'it was the human race' which crucified Christ; so 'we are present at that scene' as members of the human race; we share in this terrible responsibility and guilt: 'We dare not wash our hands . . . we are not spectators of a past event, we are in fact accomplices in a present event'. For when we meet at the Eucharist and recall that 'night in which He was betrayed' we are 'present' with Him—in that Upper Room. Here and now we are brought face to face with Christ. Of this encounter Kierkegaard says: 'I never forget this night, nor what I have understood about myself. He whom the race crucified was the Redeemer. . . . Only as saved by Him, and in His company, do I know that I shall not betray Him. . . . He was betrayed—but He was Love: in the night in which He was betrayed He instituted the Supper of Love! . . . Behold, all is now ready. He is waiting here at his holy Table—therefore do this in remembrance of Him.'[4]

Thus when we 'do this'—that is, celebrate the Eucharist— 'in remembrance' (or 'for an *anamnesis*') of Him, we are recalling an event, it is true, but we are doing more than this. For 'Jesus did not tell His disciples to remember Calvary, but to remember *Him*', that is, we are to think of Christ Crucified, it is true, but as one who 'has been crucified' and bears the marks of His passion upon Him still. Wesley and the early Methodists valued the Eucharist greatly, but 'the Sacrament could never

[3] E. L. Mascall, *Christ, the Christian, and the Church*, p. 170.
[4] S. Kierkegaard, *Christian Discourses*, pp. 286 and 288.

mean to them a bare memorial of the dead Christ, for the simple reason that He was living—still bearing upon His hands and feet glorious scars, but ascended to heaven, where He pleaded His cause with His Father for them '.[5]

Thus from the earliest days, the Christian Church has understood the Eucharist as the ' re-calling ' of Christ sacrifice, with its present redeeming power. All the early liturgies make it plain that in the worship of the Eucharist the Church is experiencing the power of the present Saviour. Past, present and future— ' Jesus Christ, yesterday, to-day and for ever '—are all gathered up and expressed in this rite, in which Christ comes to His waiting and expectant people: it is the Christ who died and rose again, who is ever interceding for us in heaven, and who will come again in power, who is here present to our adoring hearts. Prayer after prayer in the early liturgies strikes this note: ' We sinners, making the *anamnesis* of His life-giving sufferings, His saving Cross and death and burial and resurrection on the third day from the dead, and session at the right hand of Thee, His God and Father, and His glorious and terrible coming again . . . beseeching Thee that Thou wouldst not deal with us after our sins . . .'[6]

' Wherefore having in remembrance His Passion, death and resurrection from the dead, His return into heaven, and His future second appearance, when He shall come with glory and power to judge the quick and the dead . . . we offer to Thee this Bread and this Cup.'[7] ' Commanding also, and saying to them, These things as oft as ye shall do, ye shall do them in memorial of Me: ye shall preach My Death; ye shall announce My Resurrection: ye shall hope for My Advent, till again I shall come to you from heaven.'[8]

The Church of South India carries on this early tradition in its new Liturgy. Immediately after the words of Institution the worshippers say together:

Thy death, O Lord, we commemorate. Thy Resurrection we confess, and Thy second coming we await. Have mercy upon us.

Then the officiating minister continues:
' Wherefore, O Father, having in remembrance the precious

[5] Rattenbury, *The Eucharistic Hymns of the Wesleys.*
[6] *Liturgy of St. James.*   [7] *Liturgy of St. Clement.*   [8] *Ambrosian.*

death and passion and glorious resurrection and ascension of Thy Son our Lord, we Thy servants do this in remembrance of Him as He hath commanded, until He comes again, giving thanks for the perfect redemption which Thou hast wrought for us in Him.'[9]

For it is 'Me', the whole Christ, not only the victim of Calvary, which the Eucharist recalls. Thus this word *anamnesis* (remembrance) brings the Upper Room and the fact of Calvary into the present. All that Christ is, all that He has done, and all that He will do, is expressed in this Sacrament.

II

Yet though in one sense time seems to be telescoped in this rite, in another sense the element of 'time' is very significant. For every celebration of the Eucharist reminds us that our faith is based upon historic fact. It is that fact that the Eucharist makes present: the fact of Christ's sacrifice. But here it is presented to us in its true meaning: not as the pathetic death of a young prophet, hounded down by his enemies, but as the mighty act of redemption, in which evil has been conquered and the way to God thrown open for all humanity, past, present and to come. It is an historic fact that we commemorate when we obey our Lord's 'last and kindest word':

> *What He did at supper seated,*
> *Christ ordained to be repeated,*
> *His memorial ne'er to cease :*
> *And, His word for guidance taking,*
> *Bread and wine we hallow, making*
> *Thus His sacrifice of peace.*

Thus our faith is based on history: not on sentiment or imagination, or on an abstract and timeless 'truth' or 'principle', but on something which God has done. In the words of C. H. Dodd: 'It is of fundamental importance that here we have a perpetual witness to the fact that our faith rests on history. It rests upon certain events which once took place, interpreted as an act of God achieved in and through an historical personality. In the Sacrament there is a corporate memory of the facts, going back by an unbroken chain of witness to a period earlier than any of

---

[9] *The Service of the Lord's Supper or the Holy Eucharist*, authorized by the Synod of the Church of South India, O.U.P.

our written records. Our Lord is not One whom we found "in a printed book". In a perfectly real sense we "remember" that on the "night in which He was betrayed" the Lord did this and said that. Among other things we recall the fact that He broke bread and said, "This is My Body." We "remember" Him therefore as the One who has given Himself for us in order that we may have life eternal. This "corporate memory" is an important element in Christian evidence. "Thus," says Dr. Dodd, "in face of it it is idle to set forth as the 'Jesus of History' a figure who is no more than a teacher, prophet or leader. The words lead us directly from remembrance to communion." [10]

The basis of the rite therefore is historical; this anchors our faith firmly to the rock of fact. But just as all that God does 'runs out into mystery', so what we 'recall' of Christ carries us up and away beyond history, to the present working of Christ in the heavenly world, and out to the fulfilment of God's purpose for the whole universe.

No Christian can ever regard the Eucharist as a 'mere' or a 'bare' memorial—in the sense in which we use the word. 'The recalling' (of Calvary), says Dr. Mozley, 'is a great thing; the loss comes only when the memory is made the basis of a doctrine of mere memorialism. . . . To conceive of the Holy Communion as simply a meal of remembrance is to break decisively with Christian thought about the sacraments from the time when we first came in contact with such thought.' Mere 'memorialism' is not Biblical; it is out of harmony with New Testament thought.

Where such views prevail the rite loses significance; and the lifelessness of such worship shows what has been lost. The effect on Christian life is serious: it leads to great impoverishment of the life both of the individual and of the community. Some passages in a recent book by a German scholar, Dr. Preuss, show how devastating were the results of this 'memorialist view' in Germany under the influence of rationalist thought at the end of the eighteenth century: 'If it is a good thing to remember Kant, it must be a good thing to remember Jesus!'

III

All through the centuries which have passed since the first celebrations of the Eucharist in the Early Church, this 'memorial' element has been one of the predominating aspects of the rite.

[10] N. Micklem, Ed., *Christian Worship*, p. 79.

'For as often as thou *callest to mind* this mystery,' writes Thomas à Kempis in the Middle Ages, 'and receivest the Body of Christ, so often dost thou go over the work of thy redemption, and art made partaker of all the merits of Christ. For the love of Christ is never diminished, and the greatness of His propitiation is never exhausted. Therefore thou oughtest to dispose thyself hereunto by a constant fresh renewing of thy mind, and to weigh with attentive consideration the great mystery of salvation. So great, so new, and so joyful ought it to seem unto thee, when thou comest to these holy mysteries, as if on this same day Christ first descending into the womb of the Virgin were become Man, or on the Cross did this day suffer and die for the salvation of mankind.'[11]

As we gaze thus at the Love of God, shown to us in Christ, and made known to us in this tender Sacrament, sooner or later we come to know that 'this means *me*': revelation has become personal. For here Christ is the Host:

> *Behold the Eternal King and Priest*
> *Brings forth for me the bread and wine.*

He invites each one of us—personally. In other church services —if we want to—we can evade this personal summons, but we cannot evade *this* call. When we come to the Sacrament it is like climbing a mountain, along a narow path, with sheer cliffs above and below. When we meet another traveller we cannot ignore him. We have to halt, we have to listen to what he has to say; we cannot pretend we do not know that he is there. And it is at this point that Christ says to us—as He said to Judas: 'Friend, wherefore art thou come?' and then: 'I have redeemed thee, thou art Mine.'

This personal encounter is humbling. George Herbert's poem, *Love Bade Me Welcome*, leads us into the heart of this experience:

> *Love bade me welcome; yet my soul drew back,*
> *Guilty of dust and sin.*
> *But quick-eyed Love, observing me grow slack*
> *From my first entrance in,*
> *Drew nearer to me, sweetly questioning*
> *If I lacked anything.*

[11] Thomas à Kempis, *The Imitation of Christ*, Book IV, chapter 2.

'A guest,' I answered, 'worthy to be here.'
  Love said : 'You shall be he.'
'I, the unkind, ungrateful? Ah, my dear,
  I cannot look on Thee.'
Love took my hand, and smiling did reply,
  'Who made the eyes but I?'

'Truth, Lord : but I have marred them; let my shame
  Go where it doth deserve.'
'And know you not,' says Love, 'Who bore the blame?'
  'My dear, then I will serve.'
'You must sit down,' says Love, 'and taste my meat.'
  So I did sit and eat.

MEDITATIONS ON THE PASSION
(Rabanus Maurus)[12]

I pray you therefore to reflect well upon these my words that, together with all the saints of God, you may come to understand—in so far as you can—something of the length, breadth, depth and height which are to be found in the mystery of the Lord's Passion and of His Holy Cross. Indeed, this is a great secret . . . it is His delight to reveal the mystery to those who are childlike in spirit. . . . Reflect upon it with simplicity and let it fill your thought, and this meditation will become a living fire, for to consume your soul with love for its Redeemer. . . .

In the first place, consider—if you can, and in so far as you can—the inwardness of God's love for us, the same love which remained hidden for so many years, stretching forth beyond all measure known to the mind of man, that same love which had no beginning nor will ever have an end, the love in which God the Father chose us in Christ before the foundation of the world. . . . God became incarnate for love, and in His flesh He endured so much on our behalf. . . . And here you may well pause and reflect upon the breadth of God's love. . . .

In all humility consider the stupendous love of God. For man's undeserving sake God willed to become man. For the uplifting and the ·salvation of man the All-highest chose to humble Himself unto the dust of a shameful death. . . .

[12] Abbot of Fulda and Archbishop of Mainz A.D. 788-856.

God's great wisdom was there, nailed to the Cross. God's wisdom was made at one with His love in that bitter hour. . . .

Furthermore, if little of the above has moved you, can you not remember that your heavenly Father is also your own Brother in the flesh, your loyal, loving, generous Friend, continuously intent upon doing good to your soul. So loving a Friend is He that for your unworthy sake entirely did He consent to be delivered unto death. So generous a Comrade is He that for your guilt He chose to bear the hurt in His own Body, so that all your numerous misdeeds might be blotted out by the great pardon He won.

He is truly your Friend who was scourged with many bitter stripes unto the end that in His wounds your infirmities might find their healing. . . . Unto that end did His flesh die on the Cross that He might renew you even as the wings of an eagle. . . .

Let us then pray together for His mercy and compassion. Let us turn ourselves wholly to His Cross and to Him on the Cross who lives for ever and ever. . . .

PRAYER

Almighty God, Father of our Lord Jesus Christ, who, before time was hadst willed thine only begotten Son to come down among us to put on our flesh and to endure the Cross for our salvation; we adore Thee and we give Thee thanks that Thou hast vouchsafed us to share in the Passion of Thy Son our Beloved Lord. . . . Unto Him be praise and glory for ever.

CHAPTER IV

THE SACRIFICIAL CENTRE

Let all mortal flesh keep silence, and stand with fear and trembling, and ponder nothing earthly in itself; for the King of Kings, and Lord of Lords, Christ our God, cometh forward to be . . . given for food to the faithful; and He is preceded by the angels . . . that cover their faces and vociferate the hymn: Alleluia, Alleluia, Alleluia.

LITURGY OF ST. JAMES

We render thanks to Thee, Lord our God, for that Thou hast given us boldness to the entrance in of Thy Holy place, the new and living way which Thou hast consecrated for us through the veil of the Flesh of Thy Christ.

LITURGY OF ST. JAMES

That glorious King, then, who is King and Lord of all, goes out to fight against the Prince of the world, not sheltered with a shield, nor armed with iron, but fortified and armed with His Cross, to which He is to be nailed, and on which He is to die for His friends. Coming therefore to Calvary, the appointed place, with the banner of His Cross, He chose there to erect the title of His Name, and to perform the mystery of our salvation, knowing that the Tree of His Cross was to be turned into honour and to be preached all over the world.

THOMAS À KEMPIS

Christ stretched forth His hands in His Passion, and took the world in His embrace, to show that even then a great host gathered from East and West would come beneath His wings, and receive upon their brows that most noble and august sign.

LACTANTIUS

T H E Eucharist is the meeting-place of God and man. Here the Creator 'meets' His creature—whom He has created for Himself; here the Saviour welcomes the penitent sinner; here heaven comes down to earth. But this 'meeting', so full of mercy, full of compassion, is not an easy matter. Here there is no superficial dismissal of the past—'let bygones be bygones'—here the man or woman who truly desires to come into personal relation with God is aware, as never before, both of the gulf which separates man from God, and of the 'exceeding sinfulness of sin'. Sins that did not seem so bad when measured against those of other people, stand out in their full ugliness in the light of the sufferings of the Son of God.

It is this sense of sin which, in part at least, accounts for the 'fear and trembling' with which some people approach the Sacrament. Yet all 'fear that hath torment' is taken away when we realize that the cost of bearing our sins is borne by God Himself. Here we find the meaning of sacrifice.

I

The very idea of sacrifice is repugnant to many modern people. Yet we cannot get away from it, however much we may dislike it, and try to dismiss it as 'an outworn superstition', beneath the notice of 'enlightened' people. It is true that the realities of ancient sacrifice were horrifying in the extreme; nothing is gained by denying this. It is also true that all over the world religion is connected with some kind of sacrificial practice.[1] For 'sacrifice is as wide as worshipping humanity'; think, for example, of the human sacrifices of ancient Mexico, the self-torture of the primitive tribes in Malaya, the human sacrifices offered by the wild nomad tribes of the Near East in the fifth century, or the animal sacrifices offered three times a year by the Emperor of China at the Temple of Heaven, in Peking.[1a]

Modern scholars have devoted a great deal of attention to this world-wide phenomenon of sacrifice. Many of them have come to the conclusion—on scientific and objective grounds—that behind these gruesome customs there lay a deep-seated desire to achieve something, to attain something. In other words, these sacrificial rites were not meaningless cruelty and barbarism (as they seemed to onlookers); these ignorant people, in their own

[1] Hicks, *The Fulness of Sacrifice*, p. 33.
[1a] Note 3, pp. 123ff.

crude way, were trying to reach an *end*. To sacrifice a thing is to lead it to its end. It is like 'the impact of an arrow shot from a mighty bow at the moment when it quivers in the mark. Sacrifice is an offering, yes, but only in its preparation and its drive towards the goal. Its drive is not its end. It goes to it, leads to it.'[2]

Thus the idea of sacrifice brings us back to our starting-point, to the thought of the Eucharist as the 'encounter' between God and man, 'the moment when God and man unite in the great embrace, in which God's child falls into his Father's arms, and finds there his true self'.[3] In Christian terms, sacrifice is man's return to God.

II

The idea of sacrifice, however, is not only a universal human instinct; it is deeply embedded in the thought of the Old Testament. The idea of sacrifice is not merely common to the pagan world, but also to the race which God chose as the medium of His revelation of Himself to the whole of mankind.

No explanation of sacrifice is given in the Old Testament. As an institution it is taken for granted. The one principle laid down is this: 'the blood is the life'.[4] Various efforts have been made to understand what lay behind this sacrificial system of the Jews. Some hold that 'the prevailing conception of sacrifice and offering in the Old Testament is that of a gift or a present to God'.[5] Others think that the original idea was simply a general desire to put oneself in a favourable relation with the gods.[6] Not all these Hebrew sacrifices were related to sin; some were offerings of cheerful thanksgiving. But in the main the worshippers' desire in offering sacrifice was to get rid of sin by 'covering' it; that is, to 'wipe it away' in order that nothing may come between the worshipper and God.[7]

Thus the whole of this sacrificial system was an effort to restore and maintain man's fellowship with God. In these sacrifices the worshipper *does* something: he makes them his own. Bishop Hicks, in his book *The Fulness of Sacrifice*, shows the 'common underlying plan' of these Old Testament sacrifices by summarizing the six elements of the ritual:[8]

---

[2] E. Masure, *The Christian Sacrifice*, p. 41. [3] See Note 4, p. 124.
[4] Gen. 9.4. Lev. 17.10-12. Deut. 12.23.
[5] Vincent Taylor, *Jesus and His Sacrifice*, p. 49, n. 4.
[6] Ibid., p. 50. [7] C. H. Dodd, *The Bible and the Greeks*, p. 93. [8] pp. 11-14.

(i) The worshipper 'draws near' with his victim (the word to 'draw near' is the technical term for 'approach to God');

(ii) He lays or rests his hands on the head of the victim: signifying the *dedication* of his offering;

(iii) The worshipper himself (*not the priest*) kills the victim;

(iv) The priest now takes the blood—regarded as the *life*—and offers it to God (cf. Lev. 17.6);

(v) The flesh (or part of it) is burnt, the idea being that the offering is not destroyed, but 'transformed, sublimated, etherealized, so that it can ascend in smoke to the heaven above, the dwelling-place of God';

(vi) A portion of the offering is eaten by the priests and by the worshipper.

This is of course a composite description, but it is useful, because it shows us how inclusive the rite of sacrifice was: so many meanings are gathered up in the rite as a whole. Two points emerge which are of particular interest for our subject:

(*a*) the representative character of the offering;
(*b*) the fact that the blood releases the life.[9]

It is easy to see that this Old Testament system of sacrificial worship was limited, and at certain points defective. But it did contain some valuable features. It promised communion with God, encouraged the spirit of penitence for sin, and stressed the costly nature of reconciliation with God. Still more significant is the fact that this sacrificial system suggested that the foundation of true communion with God—of a real *relation* with Him—is a surrendered will and a dedicated life; further, this system combined personal and social worship. Here again we see very clearly that the root-idea of sacrifice is that of 'life offered to God, with which the worshipper can associate himself through appropriate ritual acts'.[10]

III

In spite of the perversions and abuses connected with the sacrificial system of the Old Testament, it is obvious that it prepared the hearts of men for the culmination of their obscure longings,

---

[9] Hicks, *The Fulness of Sacrifice*, p. 177.
[10] V. Taylor, *Jesus and His Sacrifice*, p. 59.

and the fulfilment of their deepest desires, in the sacrifice of Christ.
There can be no doubt that He Himself regarded His death as a
sacrifice. Two significant sayings of His suggest this: 'the Son
of Man came not to be ministered unto, but to minister, and to
give his life a ransom for many' (Mark 10.45); and the words in
Mark 14.24 (R.V.): 'This is my blood of the covenant, which is
shed for many.'

A close study of His own words in the story of the Passion
confirms this impression. He was no helpless victim of fate. He
faced death resolutely as the culmination of His self-offering to
God which began at Bethlehem. He was convinced that in so
doing He was co-operating to the full with the will of God. He
is profoundly convinced that He 'must suffer';[11] and He does so
willingly. All through the Passion story Jesus is master of the
situation; His enemies cannot arrest Him until His 'hour' has
come.[12] He says plainly that no one is taking His life away from
Him but that He is giving it, freely: 'No man taketh it away
from me, but I lay it down of myself. I have power to lay it down,
and I have power to take it again. This commandment have I
received from my Father.'[13] He gives His life willingly because
He is obedient to the Father's Will. One of His last prayers
expresses His life-long devotion: 'Father, glorify thy name.'[14]

Jesus regarded His suffering, death and resurrection as part of
His Messianic vocation; He felt He had a mission to accomplish
—something laid upon Him which taxed Him to the utmost—
something which *must* be done if He is to fulfil the end for
which He came into the world. 'His Passion is not something to be endured; it is an achievement to which His life is
dedicated.'[15]

What was it that sustained and impelled Him to this costly
effort? to this willed and deliberate sacrifice? It was love—love
only—and love to the uttermost. His purpose was pure love,
the profound desire and purpose to heal the broken relationship
between God and man—broken by man's sin—by the breaking
of His Body and the offering of Himself in sacrifice. His love is
so great that it goes to the extreme of identification with sinful
man. Never did His love and sacrifice reach greater heights than
when He cried out on the Cross, in the darkness, 'My God, my
God, why hast Thou forsaken Me?' Yet the cloud passed, and
in His last words at the very end there is the cry of triumphant

[11] Mark 8.31.   [12] John 8.20.   [13] John 10.18.   [14] John 12.28; 17.6.
[15] V. Taylor, *Jesus and His Sacrifice*, p. 258.

achievement: 'It is completed! . . . Father, into Thy Hands I commend My spirit.'

But in His sacrifice Jesus did far more than fulfil the highest longings of His own people; He did more than fulfil the longings of all mankind. In offering Himself on the Cross He lifted sacrifice itself on to a new plane. He transformed the meaning of sacrifice, because now it is God Himself who offers it. Thus He has opened up for us all a 'new and living way' into the Presence of God.

IV

The sacrificial conception of the Eucharist was inherent in the rite from the very beginning. From the day that our Lord's judicial execution by crucifixion was interpreted in the sense of 'atonement', and therefore as sacrificial, this view was inevitable. Only a few hours before His death on the Cross Jesus had spoken the mysterious words at the Last Supper about the new Covenant 'in My Blood'. There was indeed no break; there was the sense of a new life, a new creation, a new 'access' to God through His sacrifice. Lit up by the Holy Spirit the members of the Primitive Church saw the whole life and death of our Lord as the offering which was 'deliberately broken and given in the institution of the Eucharist'. A few hours later, on the Cross, the sacrifice was complete. It cost Him all He had to give. It was a real offering and a real sacrifice, wholly handed over to God. It is the completeness of the surrender and the completeness of God's acceptance of it which constitutes the reality of the sacrifice. The victim was 'made *sacrum*'—that is, He passed wholly into the hands of the Living God.

What follows can only be told in the language of pictures: God's acceptance of Calvary reverses the power of death and leads to the victory of Easter and the Ascension; the High Priest enters heaven for us; He is given the highest rights that heaven affords; something new has happened in eternity as well as in time. He has the power of an endless life.

Here we come to the heart of the meaning of the Cross and of the meaning of the Eucharist. The two are indissolubly connected. For here in the Sacrament of the Eucharist is 'redemption itself in Christ's own Person'. This does not mean that the Sacrifice of the Cross can be repeated. That has been made once for all. The Eucharist does not begin the Redemption over again, as it were, but it takes hold of it, and communicates the fruits of Christ's sacrifice. In the Eucharist we taste for ourselves how gracious the Lord is. Here we receive the forgiveness of our sins, and new life for the future. And we know that we owe all this to our Saviour and Lord, who is also our High Priest. For His work 'did not end with His death on the Cross'. That work on Calvary was indeed a finished work, a perfect sacrifice, made once for all upon earth. Yet it was the beginning of a priesthood which goes on for ever in the unseen realm, in heaven, in the Holy Place beyond the veil, into which our High Priest entered through death, and where 'He ever liveth to make intercession for us', being continually 'touched with the feeling of our infirmities'.[16]

Thus the sacrificial death of Christ is not the end of His atoning work, but it is His victorious entrance into His heavenly ministry on our behalf.

The fact of Christ's High Priesthood is an essential part of the Christian Gospel. It is closely connected with the Eucharist. For here those of us who have received forgiveness at God's hands, and who know that we are reconciled to Him through Christ, taste the powers of the age to come. We know that this new 'access' to God which we experience, both in prayer and in the Eucharist, has been won for us by Christ's sacrificial death. The New Testament is full of the grateful and adoring sense of what Christ has done to bridge the gulf between sinful man and the Holy God. To us to-day, when the sense of distance between man and God has been greatly weakened, and we have so little sense of the Holiness of God or of the sinfulness of sin, this idea of the need for a 'bridge' may sound strange and remote. But the real world—the world where things are seen in their true light—is represented in the New Testament. And here the writers are so deeply aware of the blazing reality and holiness of God that they shrink back in awe: 'Our God is a consuming fire'. All systems of religion, it is true, try to construct 'bridges'—as we see in the world-wide instinct for sacrifice—but it is only in Christianity that a really safe and secure bridge has been built. The early Christians were deeply and humbly conscious of the unfathomable cost at which God has thrown His bridge over the abyss between Himself and man.

Although this conception of the High Priesthood of Christ may have been forgotten or ignored in some parts of the Church, the

[16] Donald Baillie, *God Was In Christ*, p. 195.

conception itself is very early. There were many interpretations of the Eucharist in the Early Church, as we know, and this variety did not diminish in the succeeding ages. But gradually one single conception emerged which gathered up all these varied ideas into one key-thought: 'That the "action" of the earthly church in the Eucharist only manifests within time the eternal act of Christ as the heavenly High Priest at the altar before the throne of God, perpetually pleading His accomplished and effectual sacrifice.'[17]

This conception is based on the thought of the New Testament: primarily as worked out in the Epistle to the Hebrews, but also implied in the later Pauline Epistles, and in the other later books of the New Testament, especially in the Book of Revelation. Westcott, commenting on the words in I John: 'We have an advocate with the Father, Jesus Christ the righteous, and He is the propitiation for our sins,' says: this represents our Lord 'as a Saviour still living and in a living relation with His people . . . He is still acting personally on their behalf . . . He uses for His people the virtue of the work which He accomplished on earth . . . the "propitiation" itself is spoken of as something eternally valid and not as past'.

This view prevailed throughout the Early Church. Over and over again, in early Christian writings, we meet the dominant conception of Eucharistic worship, as centred in the Figure of Jesus, our great High Priest, serving at the heavenly altar.

The *action* of the Eucharist is always the *action of Christ Himself*, perpetually offering Himself for the life of the world. For 'as He was Man on earth so He is still Man in heaven; as He was made like in all points to His brethren on earth, so He is one with them in heaven', for He has taken up manhood into God, and has thus become our 'merciful and faithful High Priest'.[18]

V

'We have a great High Priest': What does this mean for us to-day? The Epistle to the Hebrews will be our starting-point. All through this Epistle the burden of what the writer has to say is this: 'Do you want to understand what Jesus your Lord really is? Then think of Him as High Priest, and I think I can make you understand.'

[17] G. Dix, *The Shape of the Liturgy*, p. 251.
[18] Nairne, *Epistle of Priesthood*, p. 114.

D

'Jesus Christ is the same, yesterday, to-day and for ever.' That is the clue. We must connect all our thought of Him as our living Lord in heaven with what we know about Him from the Gospels, on earth. Whatever He was *then*, He is *now*: 'that great Shepherd of the sheep' . . . 'the Good Shepherd'. So let us think of Him as He went about Galilee 'doing good'; and as we brood over the Gospel story, we see once more His infinite love, His courtesy and His tenderness to all who needed Him: to little children and their mothers; to sick, tormented and disabled people; to the bereaved and the anxious and the sorrowful; to those who were shunned by the 'good' people round them for their gross and obvious sins or because they were unpopular and because they were 'foreigners' . . . and also to violent, passionate, degraded men and women.

The earthly life of Jesus was spent in a restricted circle. Palestine was very small, and He was a Jew living under alien rule in an occupied country. Yet as we look at Him we forget this, and see Him only as *Man*, caring greatly for persons, loyal in friendship, faithful in every relationship, always courteous and forgiving, though stern to unreal and disobedient people.

Throughout His life on earth Jesus was 'laying down His life'; in hard work at home; in the obedient acceptance of the demands of daily life; in the constant strain upon His sympathies, because He *cared* so much for people; in the pain of frequent and inevitable misunderstanding, among His friends as well as His enemies; in the endurance of all the discomforts of ordinary life—heat and noise and smells and crowds—and especially in constant contact with disease, often loathsome; in the effort to deal with blindness and ignorance; in the sight of cruelty and callousness; in wandering and uncertainty; in the pain of rejection by His own people —all this, and much more than we can know or understand, was involved in that life-long obedience which made him a 'faithful and merciful High Priest'.

Above all, He expressed His love for men in His constant intercession. His long nights of prayer, His constant withdrawals into 'desert places' were not only spent in refreshing communion with the 'Father in secret', they were also times of pouring Himself out for those whom He longed to bring back to God, for His whole aim was to 'seek and to save that which was lost'. The cost was great. Think what it must have meant to Him to pray for Simon Peter, that his faith should not fail—in the end. 'But when we do consider, we are in depths where all our thoughts are drowned.' All we know is that when He prayed thus 'virtue went out of Him'. He cared intensely. Every man or woman who came to Him with suffering or sin was another burden laid upon His heart.

As we reflect upon this way of living and of loving, we begin to see what it must have cost Him to live like this: 'never to hide Himself from any need; never to refuse to get involved with people, even the worst; to feel His task of saving sinners becoming every day heavier and more urgent; and still to keep that love which will not let us go; in a word, to bear the character of the Saviour of the world'. Even He—the Son of Man, could not carry such a burden—as Man—indefinitely. Love and courage were not lacking, but His human strength could not hold out for ever.

Then came His Passion: the Agony in the Garden; the cry of desolation on the Cross. Here we see the cost of His saving activity: the burden of our sin is being borne by God Himself. The best comment on this seems to be given to us in a few lines of a popular hymn: The Good Shepherd speaks:

> *Although the road be rough and steep*
> *I go to the desert to find my sheep.*

And the hymn goes on:

> *But none of the ransomed ever knew*
> *How deep were the waters crossed,*
> *Nor how dark was the night*
> *That the Lord passed through,*
> *Ere He found the sheep that was lost.*

It was for us that He endured all this, upheld by a great hope: 'He knew that death would not release Him from His vocation or end His work, but that it would free Him by way of Resurrection from human limitations and put all authority and power into His hands.' So it seems plain 'that He looked forward to His death—in spite of moments of shrinking—as a release into an untrammelled ministry of the Spirit'.[19]

This line of thought—which keeps close to *facts*—leads us directly to the present ministry of Jesus in the 'heavenly places', manifested on earth in the Eucharist. Having conquered death, and having won the victory over sin on the Cross, and being now

[19] W. R. Maltby, *Christ and His Cross.*

Risen, Living and Ascended, He now continues for ever His saving priestly work on our behalf: both for individuals and for the world. The veil has been rent; 'the unseen world is more real, more certain, than the seen'. Whatever our need may be, we know that 'we have a great High Priest'—One who puts Himself in our place; who understands, cares, and works for us and in us. It is through Him that we have access to God, and from that Throne there flow forth streams of redeeming energy and love.

*   *   *

Dr. Rattenbury, a Methodist minister, tells a story of his childhood which illustrates this point very vividly. He says that when he was a young child there was one of the Wesley hymns which made a profound impression upon him. It is rarely used now, and it certainly was never taught to children even seventy years ago. But the central verse has remained with him all his life:

> Five bleeding wounds He bears,
>   Received on Calvary;
> They pour effectual prayers,
>   They strongly speak for me.
> Forgive him, O forgive, they cry,
> Nor let that ransomed sinner die.[20]

As a child he often pondered over the picture these lines evoked. The wounded hands of the interceding Saviour became a great reality to him, for which he has been profoundly grateful ever since. For it is 'the picture of the Lamb of God whose wounds perpetually plead with the Father for sinful men'.

> Before the Throne my Surety stands;
> My name is written on His hands. . . .
> With confidence I now draw nigh;
> And Father, Abba, Father! cry.

But the fact that Christ is 'our Great High Priest' is not only a great strength and consolation, it is also a challenge. It incites us to make the utmost effort to respond to this call to 'ascend' to the 'heavenly places' ourselves. He is our 'great high priest' who 'hath passed through the heavens' (Heb. 4.14 R.V.). Whatever the original words may mean, Dr. McNeile suggests that this is only another way of saying that He learned 'obedience by the

[20] *The Eucharistic Hymns of the Wesleys.*

things which He suffered' (Heb. 5.8). That is, that Christ passed on from stage to stage in obedience to the will of God on earth—always becoming at each stage more completely that which God willed for Him—till He passed into heaven itself, there to appear before the Presence of God for us: our High Priest, perfectly qualified for His ministry. 'Learning obedience' does not of course suggest that Christ was ever disobedient. What the writer means is that the life of Christ on earth was a continual process of learning and doing the will of God. 'The new circumstances of each new day constitute a new call to obedience in new forms to the very day of His death, and thus was He at His death "made perfect".'[21]

Thus in all our Eucharistic worship we come to receive from Christ His own spirit of sacrifice and obedience. We come to Him not only to be forgiven, but to be strengthened to give and serve and to have the spirit of discipline. It is indeed a mockery to come regularly to receive Christ at the Eucharist and then to shrink back from any call to deny ourselves, even in the smallest ways, to be unwilling to suffer or to take our full share of hard work and responsibility and pain and disappointment. Many of us 'would like to be good' but we do not like what von Hügel calls the 'bracing cost' of eternal life. 'But,' says Dr. McNeile on this point, 'there is no other way. We cannot get one inch deeper into heaven, we cannot do anything for our own souls or for the souls of other people until we begin, in union with Christ, to appear in the presence of God, each of us, a lamb as though it had been slain': that is, as one who is *offered* up to God in sacrifice.

Thus 'if Christ has ascended, by passing through all the degrees of heaven, we must also ascend in the same way, and with Him continually dwell', here and now, day by day: continually dwelling on His Passion and on His Resurrection, continually receiving from Him power to live in His Spirit and to serve and pray as He did, in our own small measure. For that is our 'holy calling'.

'Where He is, there is the altar.'

Blessed be Thy name, O Jesus, Son of the Most High God; blessed be the sorrow that Thou didst suffer when Thy holy hands and feet were nailed to the Tree; and blessed be Thy love when, the fulness of pain accomplished, Thou didst give Thy soul into the

[21] F. D. V. Narborough, *Hebrews*, Clarendon Bible, p. 100.

Hands of the Father; so by Thy Cross and precious Blood redeeming all the world, all longing souls departed, and the numberless unborn; who now livest and reignest in the glory of the Eternal Trinity, God for ever and ever.

A Procession of Passion Prayers

Almighty and Eternal God, whose worship brake forth from the ancient sanctuary at the rending of the veil, to become the salvation and joy of the whole earth : lead us now and ever into the Holiest by the new and living way which Thou hast dedicated for us in thy Son, incarnate and crucified, our everlasting Lord : to whom, with Thee and the Holy Spirit, One God, be all honour and dominion, world without end.

Ibid

O come and let us ascribe due honour to our Saviour, who hath done great things for us, great things whereof we do and ought to rejoice. Lift up your hearts and join your voices, ye children of Grace and Redemption, and let us magnify His Name together, saying : 'We praise Thee, we bless Thee, we give thanks to Thee for Thy great glory.'

St. Anselm

CHAPTER V

THE ROYAL PRIESTHOOD (a)

*Master and Lord, Jesus Christ, O Word of God, who didst
voluntarily offer thyself, a spotless Sacrifice, upon the Cross
to God and to the Father . . . who didst kindle with the
tongs the prophet's lips, and didst take away his sins, kindle
also the perceptions of us sinners, and purify us from every
spot, and cause us to stand pure before Thy holy Altar, that
we may offer to Thee the sacrifice of praise.*

LITURGY OF ST. JAMES

D U R I N G the first three centuries of the history of the Christian
Church it was often very dangerous to be a Christian. For two
hundred years—from the reign of Nero to that of Valerian (that
is, from about A.D. 65 to 260) it was a crime to be a Christian, and
' Christian worship was in itself a capital crime '.[1] Why was this?
As we know, in those early days all kinds of slanders and
calumnies were spread about the Christians: they were accused
of committing ritual murders, of occult practices or black magic,
of so-called ' sacred banquets ' which ended in shameful orgies.
The pagan inhabitants of the towns and villages of the Roman
Empire believed all these tales, and even exaggerated them.

But the fundamental reason for the legislation against the
Church was not based on this ignorant hostility but on principle:
Christianity, with its strict monotheism and its claim for the
supreme Sovereignty of the One Holy God, could not be reconciled either with pagan religion, with its many gods, or with the
fundamental conceptions of the Roman State. Then, as now,
whenever a human authority claims supreme and sole allegiance
it becomes a crime to be a Christian. For the Church was and is

[1] G. Dix, *The Shape of the Liturgy*, p. 145.

bound to take her stand on the fact that her first and supreme allegiance is to God alone, and not to the State or the Party, or to whatever body may be in power. The very fact that the Christians did not worship the 'gods' of Rome made them 'rebels', or at least they were regarded as very suspicious characters, even before the anti-Christian laws had been enacted and enforced.

It is significant that it was not Christian *belief* that was attacked, but Christian *worship*. To the Government the test of a person's Christianity (and therefore of his criminal character) was his participation in common worship. To the State, this was treason; to the Church, worship (and this always meant the Eucharist) 'was the supreme positive affirmation before God of the Christian life'.[2] The pagan State itself recognized the principle that 'religious belief can only be finally and adequately expressed by worship'.[3]

During the Decian persecution, for instance, every Christian, and every person suspected of Christian leanings, was forced to make an act of pagan worship, such as taking part in a sacred meal, or making a libation, or performing an act of sacrifice, even of the simplest kind, such as offering a few grains of incense to the statue of the Emperor, which was tantamount to accepting the official religion of Rome. The aim of this legislation was not so much to punish the Christians as to get rid of them; hence the authorities were more concerned to make apostates than martyrs. Many Christians did make some small act of conformity which satisfied the authorities; but many did not, and there were many martyrs. After the close of A.D. 250 the persecution died down and the death of Decius put an end to it for the time being. But after a few years the struggle was renewed, and though the methods were different from those used by Decius the aim was equally clear. The new persecution under Valerian began with moderation. The first edict, issued in August 257, only affected the higher clergy, who were commanded to 'sacrifice to the gods of the Empire'; they were also forbidden to celebrate Christian worship. This was a very shrewd blow at the heart of the Church. The Emperor claimed however that he was not preventing the Christians from 'honouring their god in private'. Again, this brings out very plainly the supreme importance of public worship, and, above all, of the Eucharist. To worship as a Christian in private meant that in public one had to accept the official religion and take part in its rites. Exile and death were the fate of those

[2] G. Dix, *The Shape of the Liturgy*, p. 147.   [3] Ibid.

who refused to conform. Visits to cemeteries were also forbidden, evidently because the Christians were in the habit of praying and worshipping in these places underground. Sometimes Christians who ignored these regulations were buried alive, underground, in the very places where they had gathered for worship.

The Diocletian persecution[4] was the longest and the most severe of all the persecutions during this period, although this time the attack on Christian worship was most bitter. For nearly ten years corporate worship was almost impossible, excepting in hidden and clandestine ways; the clergy were treated so harshly that they were almost wiped out, either by death or by apostasy. The edicts of toleration of 313 only came just in time to save the Church from complete disorganization.

Even when Christians were scattered by long persecution they never forgot to come together for the Eucharist. As one of them says: 'At first they drove us out, and . . . we kept our festival even then, pursued and put to death by all, and every single spot where we were afflicted became to us a place of assembly for the Feast—field, desert, ship, inn, prison.'

Thus for two hundred and fifty years it was a criminal offence to take part in Christian worship. During these years thousands of men and women were killed, tens of thousands suffered loss and indignity and exile; while many more had to live in an atmosphere of suspicion, hostility and contempt—both from their relations and their neighbours. And all through this period 'the storm centre was the Eucharist'.

Yet all through these centuries, these ordinary men and women —who were often extremely frightened—clung to the worship of the Eucharist. They 'were prepared with open eyes to accept the risks and inconveniences they undoubtedly did encounter, just to be present at the Eucharist *together and regularly*'. Even when people were lying in prison awaiting execution, at all costs their friends would try to smuggle in a presbyter and a deacon in order that they might celebrate the Eucharist *together* (as a corporate act) before they died. Why did these men and women risk their lives in order to take part in the worship of the Church: that is, in the Eucharist?

Evidently they were convinced that fidelity to the practice of Christian worship was more important than life itself. Their fidelity was due to the fundamental conviction 'that in the Eucharist—as an *action*—they could be united with the self-offer-

[4] A.D. 303.

ing of Christ for the salvation of the world'. They felt they *had* to do this, or they would have been unfaithful to their Lord, who said: 'Do this.'

II

Such fidelity to Eucharistic worship was not due to any individualistic piety. What the Christians cared about was the Eucharist as *the corporate act of the whole Church*. This view of worship, and of the Eucharist in particular, was no new thing; it was part of the earliest teaching and life of the Primitive Church. The glorious truth of Christ's High Priesthood requires our response. In the New Testament Christians are spoken of corporately as a 'priesthood'. Very little is said to believers as individuals: 'The New Testament records the experience of a family, and the second person singular is seldom employed in apostolic grammar.'[5]

In the New Testament the Church as a whole is regarded as a 'royal priesthood'; that is, it bears the same relation to the community as a whole 'as the Jewish priesthood bore to the whole people of Israel'. The Church is 'holy': separated from the world and consecrated to God. It is 'representative': destined to bring men to God, and God to men—all men without exception. Further, the Church is priestly when she shows forth that patience, gentleness, courtesy, and willingness to suffer, which characterized her Lord. The Church is a royal priesthood in the fullest sense when she bears traces of the pastoral and priestly spirit of Christ who is both Saviour and Sufferer.

Even in the first century we find that this truth was already an essential element in the life of the Christian Church. In the Letter of Clement of Rome (A.D. 96) and his allusions to the Eucharist it is evident that here 'the Eucharist is emphatically a corporate action of the whole Christian body, in which every "order" from the layman to the bishop has its own special liturgy. . . . The Eucharist is here the vital expression towards God of what the Church fundamentally *is*, a corporate "holy priesthood", to offer up spiritual sacrifices acceptable to God

---

[5] Nairne, *Epistle of Priesthood*, p. 155. Nairne points out that Hebrews, I Peter, and Revelation form a group in which the priesthood of our Lord and of His Church is part of the subject. In I Peter the writer passes quickly from our Lord's sacrificial priesthood to His pastoral priesthood. He bears men's sins on the Cross; He fulfils Isaiah 53; His blood is sprinkled; He is Bishop and Overseer, but chiefly the Good Shepherd of the Parables.

through Jesus Christ.'[6]   Indeed the references in I Peter to the Church as a 'holy priesthood' throw a good deal of light on the Eucharistic worship of the Church in the first century.

The Eucharist is regarded *as a whole*; the whole service, with its prayers and its reading of Scripture, the preaching and the offertory, as well as the strictly sacramental features are covered by the term. The Eucharist is offered by the Church *as a whole*; that is, the whole body is priestly. All the acts of the Church in the Eucharist are invested with sacrificial significance, since they are united to the sacrifice of Christ for the whole world.[7]

This emphasis upon the Eucharist as the act of the whole Church continued until the fourth century. 'There was difference of function, but no distinction in kind between the activities of the various orders in the worship of the whole Church.'[8]   In the writings of the leaders of the Primitive Church again the prevailing view—taken for granted—is that it is '*the Church as a whole*, and not any one order in it, which " is " Christ on earth'. This was of course only the logical expression of the Pauline teaching of the Church as the Body of Christ. But as Gregory Dix points out, 'the Primitive Church took this conception with its fullest force, and pressed it with a rigour which is quite foreign to our weakened notions. The *whole Church* prayed in the person of Christ; the *whole Church* was charged with the office of proclaiming the revelation of Christ; the *whole Church* offered the Eucharist as the re-calling before God and man of the offering of Christ. . . . Christ and His Church are one, with one mission, one life, one prayer, one Gospel, one offering, one being, one Father.'[9]

III

One aspect of this wholeness of the Church is the truth of the Communion of Saints. This vital element in the inner life of the Church springs directly out of its corporate character. Wherever the Church is a living ' Body ', in the New Testament sense of the word, the Communion of Saints is a vital spiritual reality. It overflows all ecclesiastical and racial barriers and brings the most

[6] I Pet. 2.5. cf. G. Dix, *The Shape of the Liturgy*, pp. 1ff., etc.
[7] E. G. Selwyn, *The First Epistle of Peter*, p. 297; J. H. Srawley, *The Early History of the Liturgy*, p. 38.
[8] G. Dix, *The Shape of the Liturgy*, p. 12.
[9] Ibid., p. 29.

diverse elements within the Church into deep spiritual communion with one another. This is part of the meaning of the Pauline words 'in Christ'.

For instance, Romano Guardini, a German Roman Catholic scholar, writes: 'The one grace of Christ flows through them all as a single stream of life. All live by the same pattern . . . The one Holy Spirit is at work in them all.' Many people would gladly agree with this, but Guardini goes further when he says: 'Each possesses grace not merely for himself but for all the rest. He passes it on in every word, every encounter with others, every good thought, and every work of charity. Every increase of the grace he possesses . . . swells the stream of grace for all the others. . . . There is something unutterably magnificent and profound in the thought that I am to share in all the purity and fulness of supernatural life hidden in the souls of others, and it is mine too, in the solidarity of Christ's Body.'

Following this train of thought he continues: 'Not one of us knows to what extent he is living by the power of grace which flows into him through others—by the hidden prayer of the tranquil heart, the sacrifices offered up by persons unknown to him. . . . It is a community of the deepest and the most intimate forces. . . . This community transcends all boundaries. It embraces all countries and peoples. It transcends the bounds of time, for in it the past is as active as the present . . . and it extends beyond the grave.'[10]

The Eastern Orthodox Church has a very strong sense of the Communion of Saints. In its view 'when the Christian takes part in the worship of the Church he thereby takes his place in the great stream of life which flows down the centuries from Christ Himself'. 'The life-blood of the Church,' says the great Russian theologian Khomiakoff, 'is prayer for one another, and the adoration of the Lord is its vital breath.'[11] For, he insists (in another passage): 'He who is saved, is saved in the Church . . . in unity with all her other members. If anyone believes, he is in the communion of faith; if he loves, he is in the communion of love; if he prays, he is in the communion of prayer. . . . Everyone who prays asks the whole Church for intercession . . . for when a man prays it is the spirit of love which prays within him.'

[10] R. Guardini, *The Church and the Catholic*, pp. 102ff.
[11] Quoted by Heiler, *The Spirit of Worship*, p. 137.

IV

As a 'royal priesthood' the Church offers 'spiritual sacrifices' to God continually. In the Eucharist this fact is expressed chiefly in two ways: through the *Offertory*, and through the *Great Intercession* or the Supplication of the Church.

In the Early Church the offertory meant a great deal more than our present attenuated practice would suggest. Irenæus says that in the offertory 'That poor widow the Church casts in all her life into the treasury of God'. This sums up in pictorial form what this part of the rite meant. The worshippers in the early days of the Church, as we know, brought their own offerings of bread and wine for the Sacrament; they were solemnly offered at the altar, given to God, to be used; in this way the laity were giving their part in the service externally, but the 'offertory' had—and has—a deep inward meaning. It was a symbolical act. Everyone present—from the bishop down to the last confirmed member of the church—was giving himself or herself to God with the bread and wine, as God 'gives Himself to them under the same forms'. In other words, by means of these united offerings the Church *becomes* the Body of Christ. Each in his or her own order made the entire offering of himself to God as part of the whole. Thus the whole act of worship was the corporate offering of the Church, as a Body. St. Augustine, preaching to the newly confirmed at Easter, said to them: 'There *you* are upon the Table; there *you* are in the Chalice.'

It is significant that where we to-day would speak of 'the communicants' the members of the Primitive Church spoke of 'the offerers'. In those days no greater punishment could be meted out to an unfaithful Christian than to forbid him 'to offer'. The very fact that we no longer use this term, but speak rather of 'going to Communion', suggests the great changes that have taken place in church life and practice. Where the laity used to take part in a corporate act, where they 'did' something, and *gave* something, where they knew themselves to be essentially the Body of Christ in the world, as the centuries passed they became passive recipients of something 'done' by the clergy. For a time indeed the layfolk communicated very rarely. So they lost both the habit of communicating and the habit of bringing their offerings of bread and wine. They had become spectators, onlookers, 'church-goers', but they did not realize that they *were* the Body of Christ. All over the world to-day the truth of the *whole* Church as the Body of Christ is being re-emphasized, and nowhere does this find more real and fruitful expression than in the worship of the Eucharist. Indeed, it is at this point that the significance of the Eucharist for the whole of human life is most perfectly expressed: the offering of all human work (symbolized by the offering of bread and wine, the fruit of human labour), of all experience, and of all relationships, to God, for His glory. Only when the members of the Church as a whole live in this spirit will the true meaning of human life become clear, and the present unhappy gap between ' Sunday ' and ' weekday ', between an unreal worship and a practical atheism, be bridged, and overcome. The so-called ' lay ' movements which are springing up here and there in so many parts of the world to-day are an earnest of the realization of the truth that Christ is Lord of all life, and that the whole of life must be brought under His sway.

So we make this ' offering ' ' for the whole family of man '. That is why the *offertory* is followed by the *Great Intercession* ' for the whole state of Christ's Church '. In the Eucharist we ' offer all and we ask all '. It was at this point in the service that in the Early Church the names of persons for whom prayer was asked were read out: people who were ill, bereaved, in prison, in danger, in exile—with these particular intercessions were gathered up the needs of the whole world, for as Evelyn Underhill says: ' Christian intercession is the completion and the expression of self-giving.'

Thus when we join in the Supplications of the Church at the Eucharist, we know that we are welcome—that we may come with confidence to One who meets us with the utmost love and understanding. We know that He is the answer to every need: nothing is too small, nothing is too great, nothing is too hard for Him—in whose hands are all power and authority.

We know that when we do not know how to pray, when our hearts are cold and our desires confused and halting, when we cannot find words to ease the burden or the pressure upon our spirit, He takes our confused stammering efforts, and infuses into them His own warmth and reality; we can be quiet, and commit ourselves, our needs, and those of others, into His hands, for He takes our thought, interprets it, and answers it in His own way.

We know that, in spite of our sinfulness, we are received with Infinite mercy: He is our Judge, and He has authority to execute judgment *because He is the Son of Man*—and it is He who says:

'It is not the will of your Father that one of these little ones should perish.' So we can turn to Him after every failure, and meet with fresh understanding, fresh forgiveness, fresh power to go on.

Finally, He gives us hope: hope for others, for the Church, for the world. Seeing that 'he ever liveth to make intercession' we must never lose heart. However impotent we may feel—and may be—we shall have courage to go on praying and loving and serving, because *He is at work unceasingly* for the saving of the whole world.

FROM THE LITURGY OF ST. MARK

Visit, O Lord, in Thy pity and mercies, those of Thy people that are sick; those of our brethren that have departed or are about to depart; give to each a prosperous journey in his place. . . . Send down rains on the places that stand in need of them. Raise the waters of the river to their measure through Thy grace. . . .

Heal them that are vexed of unclean spirits, them that are in prisons, or in mines, or in courts of justice, or with sentence given against them or in bitter slavery. . . . Have mercy upon all; free all; . . . to every Christian soul that is in trouble give mercy, give refreshment.

FROM THE LITURGY OF ST. JAMES

For the peace that is from above, and the love of God, and the salvation of our souls, let us make our supplication to the Lord:

For the peace of the whole world, and the unity of all the holy churches of God.

For them that have desired us to make mention of them in our prayers. . . .

For them that are in old age and infirmity, the sick, the distressed, and that are vexed of unclean spirits, their speedy healing from God, and salvation;

For them that carry on their struggle in the caves and dens and holes of the earth, our holy fathers and brothers;

For Christians that sail, that journey, that are strangers, and for our brethren that are in bonds and exile and imprisonment and bitter slavery, their peaceful return.

FROM THE LITURGY OF ST. CLEMENT

For them that sail and that journey
Let us make our supplication:

*For them that are in mines and exiles and prisons and bonds for
the Name of the Lord,
Let us make our supplication:
For our enemies and them that hate us for the Lord's sake,
Let us make our supplication:
For them that travail in bitter slavery,
Let us make our supplication:
For them that are without and wandering,
Let us make our supplication:
That the Lord may convert them;
For every Christian soul,
Let us make our supplication.*

CHAPTER VI

THE ROYAL PRIESTHOOD (b)

Jesus our Brother, Jesus the Man . . . Jesus the representative of our race before the Throne of God, His and our Father, stood and stands before that Throne in the character of Priest . . . Jesus by taking upon Himself the priesthood, caught up this very ancient thing (sacrifice) and gave it real meaning, power and value. He is still the Priest, and we are His instruments. We are not each separate 'priests' but the 'Priest' Christ, by sharing with Him, our action being most truly His action. In our priestly life we distribute Christ's gifts, we share in His sacrifice. When we come to die, our death will be sacrificial, the consummation of our sacrifice . . . for Christ is living and dying in us.

COLUMBA CARY ELWES, O.S.B.

'I BESEECH you therefore, brethren, by the mercies of God, to present your bodies a living sacrifice, holy, acceptable to God, which is your reasonable service'; or, as in the Moffatt translation: 'I appeal to you by all the mercy of God to dedicate your bodies as a living sacrifice, consecrated and acceptable to God: that is your cult, a spiritual rite.' These great words of St. Paul make explicit the claim that the whole life of the Christian is intended by God to be sacrificial. He is urged to lay his body —his personality as a whole—as a *living sacrifice* upon the altar of God. In other words, the 'spiritual sacrifices' which the Church offers must be completed in the lives of the members of the Body of Christ. It is not enough to join, however sincerely, in the worship of the actual rite of the Eucharist; here St. Paul claims—as he does elsewhere—that 'the whole life of Christians is a sacrificial life'. St. Paul himself lived this out in his own life: he regarded all his missionary work as a sacrificial offering to

E

God (Rom. 15.16); writing from prison, where he was waiting for his trial, where death might come at any moment, he thinks of his life as a sacrifice, freely and willingly offered: 'Even if my life-blood has to be poured as a libation on the sacred sacrifice of faith you are offering to God, I rejoice, I congratulate you all—and you in turn must rejoice and congratulate me' (Phil. 2.17. Moffatt). When his martyrdom seems imminent, he writes: 'The last drops of my own sacrifice are falling; my time to go has come' (II Tim. 4.6. Moffatt).

Throughout the New Testament it is evident that the whole Christian life is intended to be an oblation, an offering to God for His glory, and for the good of the Church and the world; this conception covers everything, so that even the gifts sent by the Philippians to St. Paul in Rome, and the songs of praise and the good deeds of the Hebrews are regarded as 'sacrificial'.

Echoes of these great words of St. Paul occur like a refrain in the early liturgies. For instance, in the Liturgies of St. Mark, St. James, St. Basil and St. Chrysostom (to name only four) the phrase 'reasonable service' occurs in different contexts. It is always used in a spiritual and sacrificial sense, of the offering of the worshippers' whole lives in praise and obedience.

A priestly life of this kind is the fulfilment and the transformation of the ancient idea of sacrifice. It is derived from, inspired and maintained by the Eucharist. For, as Dr. Dodd says in his commentary on Romans: 'The language of sacrifice expresses figuratively a reality which is personal and ethical. . . . In speaking of the Sacrament of the Lord's Supper Paul can say *The cup of blessing which we bless, is it not a communion of the blood of Christ* (I Cor. 10.16), i.e., participating in His life as dedicated to God.' So as Christians we are called to live 'priestly' dedicated lives, wherever we may be and whatever our work in the world may be. Such a conception of life will, and must inevitably, find outward expression. But here we are thinking mainly of the inward side, of the spirit of 'priestly' service which springs directly out of our practice of worship, and supremely from the worship of the Eucharist.

The power of a 'priestly' life depends mainly upon the reality of our hidden offering, on the way in which we accomplish our 'reasonable service'. This secret offering is made in three ways: in prayer, in suffering, and in the service of love.

II

The priestly service of prayer comes first. Here we need the constant reminder that there is no contrast between the corporate worship of the Church—with its centre in the Eucharist—and our personal practice of prayer. In the Eucharist both the personal and the corporate aspects of prayer meet and blend. So even in our most ' private ' prayers we are really praying in and with the Church. 'Indeed, it is only as a member of the Body that the Christian can pray *Christian* prayer at all; for Christian prayer is Christ's own prayer communicated to us.'[1] What does this mean? How can we share in ' Christ's own prayer '? To some of us the phrase may sound obscure or unreal. A little reflection, however, shows that this truth is one of the fruits of the Incarnation. Because God became Man, and manhood has been taken up into God, Christ represents in His own Person the whole of humanity. Therefore the whole of His human experience, all that He suffered and endured, in some way influences the life of everyone, until time shall end.

This is effected through His High Priesthood. He is always ministering at the heavenly altar. He wills that we too should share in this ' duty and service '. As Irenæus says: ' Thus also He wills that we in our turn should offer oblation at the altar often and without intermission. For there is an altar in heaven; for thither are our prayers and oblations directed.' We can only do this as we are united to Christ, and He gives us His own life, which enables us to pray and give and sacrifice. United with Him, our Great High Priest, we are ' wired ' both to God and man.

This ' priestly ' prayer however, as we have already said, is always part of the prayer of the Church. In the words of Father Andrew, ' There is really only one prayer to God and that is the one prayer of the one Son to the Father; our prayer is only real prayer as it is taken into that prayer.' We never approach God in prayer alone. We are unique and personal, it is true, and we may have very different ' callings ' in prayer, but our service of prayer must always be offered within the reality of the community of Christians all over the world, and all down the ages.

As members of the ' royal priesthood ', we take our part in the great work of bringing the world back to God. The much mis-

[1] Mascall, *Christ, the Christian, and the Church*, p. 205.

understood phrase, the 'priesthood of believers' here gains its true meaning. We offer our prayers not as a number of detached individuals, nor for a number of other individuals in whom we may be interested, but as part of the 'full Christian priesthood of believers'. This 'priesthood' becomes fully effective only as it is part of the life of the priestly Body—the Body of Christ. In the first place this priestly office is exercised through intercession.

It is a very wonderful thing that God has given us the power to offer loving prayers which are effective in helping others, which actually lift them up into God's presence. When we enter into the ministry of intercession we become transmitters of the redeeming transforming grace of God. Were this to depend upon ourselves, upon the energy of our prayers, upon our love—a very imperfect thing as we know only too well, we could not offer this service; we could not be 'priestly' souls. But here we come back again to the basis of all prayer, and of this kind of prayer in particular, to the prayer of Christ, our Great High Priest. To quote Father Andrew again: 'There is only one true prayer to God and that is our Lord's intercession; our prayer is only true prayer to the degree in which it is one with His. The more simple and silent your prayer is, the more will it be taken into our Lord's prevailing intercession.'

Connecting our personal intercessions for the world, for the Church, for special causes, and for particular people, with the Eucharist, means that we are supported by the knowledge that we are part of the communion of saints; further, we know that all prayers and self-offering have a real effect in the hidden world of persons, even though we may never see any results. This priestly work of prayer demands great faith and courage. It is not easy to go on praying believingly without seeing any change in a situation. Yet surely here—in the mystery of apparently un-answered prayer—we are encouraged when we think of our Lord's prayers for His disciples and especially for Judas. This kind of prayer, as someone has said, 'is like a temple. To enter the outer court is not so difficult and to stand in the holy place is always possible to devout souls; the Holy of Holies is a place of priestly sacrifice, and many truly earnest souls shrink from its exacting demands and seek to persuade themselves that the altar is not everyone's vocation. But in the temple of prayer, as in every temple, it is the altar that interprets and sanctifies the whole.'[2]

[2] E. Herman, *Creative Prayer*, p. 215.

We need more than courage and fortitude, however, if we are to take our part in this priestly service: we need preparation. So often we feel uneasy about our prayers of intercession and 'wonder whether after all it's any good', because we have not entered upon this 'exercise'—as our Puritan forefathers used to say—without deliberate and thoughtful preparation. Aaron, the type of all priests, could not enter the sanctuary for any priestly service without preparation. Outside the sanctuary stood the Laver, the large basin in which the priests washed their hands and feet. Thus any deeper exercise of prayer and especially prayer for the interests of God, and the need of the world, requires the preparation of cleansing: sorrow for sin, confession, and forgiveness. We may indeed be finding public worship and personal prayer difficult because of some habit or some sin which is hindering us. We may know ourselves well enough to have some idea of the reason for our inner dissatisfaction. When we realize further that we are members of a 'royal priesthood' and that we are called to represent mankind before God, we realize that our sins do not merely spoil our own lives and hinder our own prayers, but that they are an injury and a wrong to mankind. 'Every Christian who is trying to be holy for the sake of others knows that an immeasurable responsibility attaches to his sin.'[3] So full confession and acknowledgement of our sin, together with all the practical amendment to which this leads, is necessary, if we are to intercede as we should. We must then with firm faith receive the forgiveness of God, and go forward resolutely to take upon us the full weight of our vocation. 'The laver of divine washing is the first absolute necessity of our priesthood.'[4]

After the preparation of cleansing, Aaron moved on to the Holy Place. But before he entered it he passed the Altar of Burnt-offering. At this altar the blood of the animal sacrifice was poured out, to show that the 'life' was given to God, while the body was given by being burnt. The whole animal was given to God in this way, and that is why it was called a 'whole burnt offering'. A further element in our preparation for priestly service is that of self-surrender. That is why St. Paul lays so much emphasis upon 'wholeness': 'The God of peace himself sanctify (consecrate) you *wholly*; and may your spirit and soul and body be preserved *entire* . . .' (I Thess. 5.23 R.V.). This is the work of a life-time, and needs to be renewed again and again. But in

[3] A. H. McNeile, *Devotion and Discipleship*, p. 419.   [4] Ibid.

principle at least, we must be continually aiming at this ever deeper giving of ourselves to God that He may use us as He wills.

The essence of intercession is vicarious offering. For intercession is a root-principle of Christian living. It is part of the life of the Body of Christ, who prayed on the eve of His Passion: 'For their sakes I consecrate myself'. Here is a description of the spirit of this kind of intercession which sums up all that needs to be said on this point:

'If I bear my sinful brother, as Christ took our sin upon Himself, and ever confess his misery as my own, and pray for mercy and grace, that God in Christ may look down upon me and help me to bear my brother's sin and give me his soul, then I am a priest of God. This royal priesthood is a very deep mystery, and those who bear this office are pupils under God's immediate eye, and His beloved children, who enter into the Holiest of Holies. . . . They enter the strife for their brethren, and help them by prayer, and by the offering up of their life for them, that they may overcome. The soul that is anointed for the priesthood of Christ must thus fill up what remains of the sufferings of Christ.'[5]

In practice, do we need *method* if we are trying to practise this kind of prayer? To some extent we do. Dr. McNeile suggests that 'prayer is a gift to God, like an incense offering', and thus that when the Psalmist said 'Let my prayer be *set forth* in Thy sight as the incense', he was using a technical expression which denotes the 'arranging and setting in order of a sacrificial offering'. So that these words really mean: 'Let my prayer be got ready, arranged, set in order.' Whether in our 'intentions' at the Eucharist or in our personal intercessions we shall pray better —with a quieter mind and a clearer purpose—if we take some trouble to think about our prayers beforehand. In a sense it is not even reverent to come unprepared to this service.

At the same time, provided we have made the needful preparation, the simpler we are the better. We shall pray as the Spirit leads us: sometimes pouring out our hearts in words and desires; sometimes remaining still in the presence of God. Once we have begun to realize the vast redeeming power of our Lord's unceasing intercession, the stream of love and power and energy which is ever flowing forth from the 'Throne of grace', it will often be enough for us to lay the particular need 'in the stream

[5] John G. Gichtel.

of our Lord's will and re-creating love which flows everywhere and at all times, and leave Him to deal with it'. We know that such prayer is never wasted. We know that our Lord accepts our offering and will use it as He wills. Effective intercession is controlled by *God*, and not by our human ideas and desires; hence it is essential that we should always prepare for it by worship, and by giving our minds to God and His power, rather than by being exclusively absorbed in the human side of the matter. In the words of Father Andrew: 'There is no intercession like the prayer of silent adoration. Intercession is *not* giving God information, or reminding Him, or making suggestions. It is just putting the riches of our love at the disposal of His. Into the ocean of His love flows the rivulet of yours, and His love operates through yours.'

So as we give ourselves to Him for His use, and our prayers (which may seem very weak and ignorant) united with His continual intercession, are gathered up and used by Him, we in our turn become instruments for the healing and saving of the world. For He is able to save to the uttermost all who come unto God through Him.

Lilias Trotter, a great missionary of a previous generation, who lived and worked and prayed for the Muslims of North Africa, was full of the encouragement that this truth of Christ's priesthood gave her in her difficult and discouraging work. In one place she says: 'Out of the midst of deadness or coldness we step instantly, as if it were the next room, into the holiest sanctuary in the universe, where God is shining all around and in an utter stillness we can hear His voice' (Heb. 10.19). Again: 'All the sense of helplessness and failure over prayer is only meant to make way for the prayer-life of Christ in us, and a fellowship with Him in which it will "make all things new". . . . What might not our prayer power be if it came down from the Throne of the Priest, linked with His prayer. Let us believe it and then act our faith. And the impossible will become possible and the invisible will come into sight.'

III

Another element in the 'priestly' life of the members of the Body of Christ is *suffering*. By 'suffering' we mean every kind of trial: loss, sorrow, bereavement, loneliness, pain of body and mind, limitation of all kinds, frustration, disappointment, injustice, oppression—in short, every human experience which hurts us, everything which 'touches us on the raw', everything from which we instinctively want to escape. This includes trials incurred in defence of our convictions, or in loyalty to Christ, but it is not confined to such kinds of suffering.

For most of us this is a very practical problem. Whatever our theory may be, and however 'intellectual' we may be, we all have to live. How can we, as Christians, and as members of a 'royal priesthood', deal with pain creatively? As Christians we claim that since Jesus won the victory over sin on the Cross and rose again His followers have shown in every age that it is the supreme glory of the Christian way of life that it is able to deal with the problem of pain on the practical plane of daily living.

How then are we to turn the ordinary experiences of pain or suffering that may come to any of us into 'spiritual sacrifice'? Certainly we cannot do it all at once. 'For,' as von Hügel says, 'to suffer well is far more difficult than to act well.' It is indeed very difficult. The initial stages leading to complete acceptance are often very long, with repeated revolts and despairs; we may think we have reached the goal, and then some slight incident or suggestion will cause such an upheaval that the whole battle has to be fought over again. Yet sooner or later, by the help of God, we come through to a breathing-space, and find a measure of peace.

This 'acceptance' is a very different matter from 'setting one's teeth' or 'trying to grin and bear it', admirable though such courage is. It is also very different from that sickly 'resignation' which infects so many hymns and verses of a certain type; such 'resignation' is in point of fact a kind of inverted rebellion! For it suggests that God is *not* good nor is He wise, since all we can do is to 'endure' His dealings with us—a most un-christian attitude!

The *Selected Letters* of von Hügel are full of glimpses of his own attitude to suffering, an attitude which was wise, bracing and profoundly Christian. Writing to a friend who was very ill, he says: 'I was so very glad to get your letter, and to see from that . . . the devotedly straight, simple and humble way in which you are taking your great trial, thus turning your "passion" into an action, and what of itself only sours or revolts into a sweetening and strengthening of the soul. L—— told me of the help you were finding in the Gospels and in the *Imitation*. How almost purely literary their effect is upon us, when we are not suffering, or (at least) when we have not suffered—*and much*. But when penetrating pain comes, and if we can only try to meet straightly and severely those bitter waters, then those books cease to be so much writing—they become alive with Christ our Life, Who . . . brings Life and Love in and through the Cross.'[6]

Again, in answer to a request for further advice, he suggests actual ways of dealing with attacks of pain: 'Try more and more, *at the moment itself*, without any delay or evasion, as simply, as spontaneously as possible, to cry out to God, to Christ our Lord, in any way that comes most handy, and the more variously the better. "Oh! this is real. Accept it, as a little real atonement for real sin!" "Oh! help me to move on, from finding pain so real to discovering sin to be far more real." "Oh! May this pang deepen me, may it help to make me real—really humble, really loving, really ready to live or die with my soul in Thy hands!" . . . And so on, and so on. . . . The all-important point is to make such ejaculations *at the time* and *with the pain well mixed up into the prayer*.'[7]

Such acceptance, which is itself an activity, an energy of heart and will, leads on to the further conviction that *suffering is action*. Speaking of the recent death of his daughter Gertrud, von Hügel says: 'When we first got to Rome, she was wonderfully plucky and courageous, "grinning and bearing", a dear stoic. But then gradually she became . . . more and more sensitively Christian. The Cross became, not simply a fact, to bear somehow, as patiently as we can, but a source and channel of help, of purification and of humble power—of a permanent deepening, and sweetening of the soul . . . Suffering can be the noblest of all actions.'[8]

Sometimes such 'action' will totally transform a given situation: leading to healing of body and mind (where the suffering is due to physical or mental causes), or turning what looked like final defeat into something so rich and fine that it seems a miracle. Such experiences are very costly, but they are invaluable, not only for ourselves, but for others. For they are creative: acceptance of the will of God, in darkness and blindness, seeing no way out, has become co-operation with His creative energy, and something *new* has been born.

From such a creative attitude to suffering, it is not far to the

[6] Friedrich von Hügel, *Selected Letters*, pp. 227-228.
[7] op. cit., p. 231.   [8] op. cit., p. 227.

final stage—where suffering is willingly borne for others—offered to God for His redeeming purpose in the Church and in the world. Here the sacrificial life, incumbent on all members of the Body of Christ, reaches one of its highest points. Again, von Hügel speaks out of his own experience when he writes thus to his niece: 'I wonder whether you realize a deep, great fact? That souls—all human souls—are deeply interconnected? That we can not only pray for each other, but *suffer* for each other?' Then he goes on to speak of his trying state of health, and of what it meant to him to be able 'to offer it to God and to Christ for my child—that He might ever strengthen, sweeten, steady her in her . . . dependence upon Him'. 'Nothing,' he continues, 'is more real than this interconnection—this gracious power put by God Himself into the very heart of our infirmities . . . and it is the Church, which at its best and deepest, is just *that*. . . .'[9]

All who have really suffered—in mind, body or estate—know that the hardest element in all suffering is not the actual pain (most people have a great deal of courage and dignity) but the apparent waste: the sense of futility, of emptiness, of uselessness. To be condemned to external inaction, to be confined within narrow limits, to be unable to use natural gifts, or to be denied some very human and natural outlet: in whatever form such trials may come, this is the aspect which embitters or depresses those who have to endure them. And it is this creative use of suffering as *action* and as *sacrifice* which transforms it. When we can offer ourselves to God so completely that the 'dedicated life' of Christ is actually communicated to us—we are very near to God, the heart of reality.

The history of the Church is full of such self-offering. In times of persecution the inward 'sacrifice', which is our 'reasonable service', was often completed (as in the case of St. Paul and in the Early Church as a whole) by the loss of freedom, by pain of body, and finally by martyrdom. Such sacrifices have been made all down the centuries, and they are still being offered to-day.

But for most people the 'spiritual sacrifice' is made within—in heart and will—and is usually known to God alone. All that others see is a certain joy and serenity, a sureness in dealing with adverse conditions, which sometimes causes astonishment, but more often is taken for granted. The deep meaning of it all lies

[9] Friedrich von Hügel, *Selected Letters*, p. 269.

in the hidden personal life of worship and dedication. Such persons rarely reveal in words the sources of their strength, but they give freely to others, and they have much to give. Here are two examples of this kind of 'creative living', characteristic of the 'priestly' life.

The first is that of a young Swiss girl, Adèle Kamm, a member of the Swiss Reformed Church. She was born at Lausanne in 1885. At the age of nineteen she was struck down with a very painful kind of tuberculosis. Her engagement had to be broken off. After several efforts to get well it became plain that she would not recover. Through much difficulty she adjusted herself to the prospect of suffering and death, and in spite of great suffering she led a creative life, full of joy, and full of service to others. 'Life and death,' she wrote towards the end of her short life, 'are alike joy to me.' She died at Geneva at the age of twenty-six. In her effort to adjust herself to her lot she passed through all the stages of despair, revolt, depression, to acceptance, and then on to suffering as 'action' and as 'sacrifice'. Writing to a friend two years before she died, Adèle says: 'Until now I have always taken care to hide the secret of my joy in suffering in the deepest recesses of my soul. Faith, and love of God in Christ, can give the only consolation to those in affliction, but I believe the source of abiding joy in constant suffering lies in a somewhat vague, confused, but real sense of vicarious sacrifice.' She was greatly encouraged to have this dim but very real conviction confirmed by a book in which the writer makes it explicit by connecting it with those mysterious words of St. Paul: 'I rejoice in my sufferings for your sake, and fill up on my part that which is lacking of the afflictions of Christ in my flesh for his body's sake, which is the Church' (Col. 1.24).

Adèle Kamm was no theologian, but she had penetrated deeply into the meaning of the Christian faith. She believed that her suffering, willingly accepted, was already being used by Christ for His redeeming purpose: 'We also suffer with, and on behalf of each other. . . . All of us suffer in some way, but some have to bear a double portion, for the sake of those who suffer less—the innocent child for the criminal, the elect for the depraved. . . . We continue the work of Christ in miniature. . . . Should not we human beings, who are bound to each other by the ties of common brotherhood, be glad and willing to give ourselves to suffer for each other? . . . There, my dear friend, you have the secret of the faith which strengthens me to go forward with courage, and makes my present life of suffering far happier than the former one. . . . I rejoice to know that in a quiet way my life is being used for the good of the race.'[10]

The second example comes from France. Elisabeth Leseur (1866-1914), was a Parisian lady, whose life followed a very different course from that of the young Swiss Protestant. Outwardly, her life seemed destined to be very ordinary. She came from an educated middle-class family. Her parents were Catholics, but not particularly ardent ones. Elisabeth learnt her Catechism, was confirmed and became a ' practising Catholic ' like all the other young girls of her circle. Religion at that time was not a matter of great moment to her, but she held to the external forms as a matter of course. She developed into a charming, cultivated woman of the world, in the best sense. She had keen enjoyment of all that intellect and art could offer. She knew several languages: Latin, English, Russian, and Italian.

In her early twenties, she married Felix Leseur, a brilliant young agnostic whose interests were mainly intellectual and political; further, he was a convinced anti-clerical. The Leseurs' new home soon became a social centre for politicians of the Left, publicists, journalists, medical men, professors, scholars, musicians, writers and artists. Elisabeth took her place easily and naturally in this society, and was a charming hostess; both she and her husband went out a great deal into society. Elisabeth had no children, which was a sorrow to her, but it left her free to cultivate her mind, and to do everything with her husband. They travelled a great deal—in Spain, Italy, North Africa, the Near East, Greece, Germany and Russia.

Many sorrows and anxieties, and finally illness and prolonged ill-health came to Elisabeth. From 1908 to 1912 she was forced to lead a very restricted existence. From 1912 the cloud of ill-health deepened; after a period of great physical suffering she died on the 3rd of May, 1914, at the age of forty-eight. These are the bare facts of her external life. It was what she made of them which makes her remarkable. Soon after their marriage Felix Leseur became annoyed with his wife for her adherence to religion and to the Church. Although he had promised to ' respect her convictions ' while they were engaged, he became so·impatient with her that he tried his hardest to shake her faith. For a time it seemed as though he would succeed. He persuaded her to give up going to church, and at that time her faith was

[10] P. Seippel, *A Living Witness*, E. T. O. Wyon.

severely shaken. Then, thinking that this would complete the 'good work', he gave Elisabeth Renan's *Vie de Jésus*. It had the opposite effect. She was not impressed by Renan, but the reading of this work sent her to the Gospels. She read and studied them as never before. She set herself to seek God, and after a long solitary search, with no human being to help her, she became a deeply convinced Christian. Her position was a very difficult one: she loved her husband deeply and he was an ardent unbeliever. Almost all the people she met were hostile mocking intellectuals. She had to carry on her 'society' life, entertain, and go out, and dress well, and yet at the same time lead a Christian life. She succeeded in a remarkable way, but her deepest life had to be hidden. Her life was nourished by prayer, the Bible, and the Eucharist. She confided her thoughts and prayers to a *Journal*, which was published after her death. A few weeks after she died her husband was fully 'converted' and her papers were published by him; they have been a help to thousands of people in many lands, for they have been translated into several languages.

Suffering came to her in many ways: there was the spiritual loneliness which was inevitable, much sorrow and anxiety, as well as a great deal of actual pain and discomfort. Her deepest sorrow of all was her apparent failure, in spite of all her prayers, to win her husband to the Christian faith. To herself, she seemed to have achieved nothing.

Her *Journal* reveals the secret of her serenity and courage. Her husband had already been greatly impressed by her attitude to suffering. 'More and more,' he wrote later on, 'I wondered at and admired her moral force in the midst of physical agony.' She knew what she was doing however; here are her own words about it:

'There are moments in life when we should look neither backwards nor forwards, nor to either side, but solely contemplate the Cross, that which God offers to us and from which will flow great graces, both for ourselves and for others. I know what suffering means, the wonderful and mysterious power it possesses, what it achieves and what it accomplishes. In reality our action is a very small thing. . . . Therefore when it pleases God to use suffering (rather than action) to carry on His work, I believe that we ought not to be too sorry for ourselves, for we may then be sure that the work will be well done, and that it will not be mingled with all that wretched egotism and pride which sometimes spoil our external activity. I know by experience that certain graces were obtained for others during the hour of trial, graces which we could not gain before with all our efforts. Thus I have come to this conclusion, that suffering is a higher form of action, the highest expression of the Communion of Saints, and that in suffering one is sure of being freed from self-deception, sure also of being useful to others, and to the great causes one so longs to serve.'

Both prayer and suffering then are vital elements in the life of the 'royal priesthood', and are the sources of all creative and saving activity. But the whole of life is to be offered to God with all its experiences. There is nothing except sin which God cannot and will not use. It is this attitude of loving worship which transforms life and makes it our 'reasonable service', as we joyfully co-operate with the perfect and acceptable will of God. Then we can pray with the Psalmist:

> O send out Thy light and Thy truth; let them lead me . . .
> Then will I go into the altar of God,
> Unto God my exceeding joy.

We beseech Thee, O Lord, remember Thy Holy Catholic and Apostolic Church, from one end of the world unto the other, and give peace unto it, which Thou hast purchased with the precious Blood of Thy Christ, and strengthen this holy House till the consummation of the world. Remember, O Lord, them who have offered their holy gifts unto Thee, and those for whom, or for what ends they have offered them. Remember, O Lord, them who bring forth fruit, and do good works in Thy Holy Churches and who remember the poor. . . . Remember, O Lord, those in deserts and mountains and caves of the earth. . . . Remember, O Lord, the people who stand around, and those who are absent and have mercy upon them and upon us, according to the multitude of Thy mercy. . . . Remember, O Lord, them that are in trials and banishments, and all tribulation and necessity and distress and all that need Thy great loving kindness. Free those troubled by unclean spirits; sail with them that sail; journey with travellers; protect widows and orphans, deliver the captives, and heal the sick. . . . Pour out on all men Thy rich mercy, granting to all their petitions unto salvation. And those whom we, through ignorance, or forgetfulness, or the number of names, have not remembered, do Thou, O God, remember them, who knowest the age and the name of each one, who knowest each from his mother's womb. For Thou, O God, art the Help of the helpless, the Hope of the hopeless, the Saviour of the tempest-tossed, the Harbour of mariners, the Physician of the sick. Be Thou Thyself all things to all men, who knowest each, and his petition and his dwelling and his need.

LITURGY OF BASIL THE GREAT

CHAPTER VII

HOLY COMMUNION

―――――

LORD, this is Thy feast,
prepared by Thy longing,
spread at Thy command,
attended at Thine invitation,
blessed by Thine own word,
distributed by Thine own hand,
the undying memorial of Thy sacrifice upon the Cross,
the full gift of Thine everlasting love,
and its perpetuation till time shall end.
LORD, this is Bread of heaven,
Bread of life,
that, whoso eateth, never shall hunger more.
And this the Cup of pardon, healing, gladness, strength,
that, whoso drinketh, thirsteth not again.
So may we come, O Lord, to Thy Table;
Lord Jesus, come to us.

THE Communion completes the action of the Eucharist. It is the communion of the faithful with Christ and with each other. This final action is the climax of the whole act of worship. To many sections of the Christian Church this one aspect of the Eucharist is so wonderful and so glorious that all the other aspects fade into insignificance. When this takes place, the whole meaning of the rite consists in the giving and receiving of the Living Bread: 'Eucharist, with its emphasis on the adoration of God, vanishes. Communion, with its emphasis on man's need, takes its place.'[1] Such a view, however, ignores the fact that 'communion is the fruit of sacrifice', and it destroys the ancient pattern of the Eucharist, which has been preserved from the very earliest days of the Church, a pattern which was not imposed

[1] E. Underhill, *The Mystery of Sacrifice*, p. 58.

upon the act of worship but which grew out of it naturally and inevitably.

In the previous chapters we have been thinking about the different strands of meaning which blend in this great 'mystery' of Christian worship. When we look at the service as a whole, however, we can see that there is an order—or a pattern controlling the whole; this is what an artist would call its 'significant form'. Behind this 'pattern' is the one all-inclusive basic fact: *God gives*. All human worship is our response to the love of God. In the end all our thoughts of God come back to this: that God is Love, and that He is always giving Himself.

So when we speak of a 'pattern' of worship we do not mean anything complicated or difficult. All we are saying is this: God gives; we respond. The action of the Eucharist consists in this two-way relationship between God and man. This is only another way of saying: 'God made us for Himself, and when we offer real worship we come back to Him.' It is all very simple—and very deep. God loves and God gives. God calls and we answer; God asks our love and we give it back to Him. The human aspect of the Sacrament is our response to the outpouring of God's sacrificial love. In every celebration of this Sacrament God makes a fresh appeal to our hearts; He gives Himself afresh to our hungry souls.

The pattern is plain enough: in the *Preparation* we realize our unfitness to receive the gift of God; we confess our sins, receive forgiveness, and listen to the proclamation of the Gospel; then we offer ourselves with our gifts at the *Offertory*, in union with the perpetual self-offering of our Great High Priest, followed at once by the sacrifice of *Intercession* for the whole world for which Christ died. Then comes the great *Prayer of Consecration*, when all we can give is offered up in faith and love to the Triune God in His fulness; He accepts and uses what is given, and in His turn prepares to give Himself to His waiting children. This is the moment of *Communion*: the climax and the completion of the whole.

'Communion is the fruit of sacrifice': we have offered our small and imperfect gifts—we have done what we were able—and the love of God, in infinite mercy and gentleness, takes what is offered, consecrates and transforms it. Thus the act of Communion should never be separated from the whole act of worship in the Eucharist. Indeed, we shall miss the deeper significance of this precious moment of *Communion* if we are

F

not aware of the preceding moment of *Consecration*. For all
through the Eucharist what matters is the Glory of God, the
Will of God, the fulfilment of the purpose of God, not the satisfaction of our human needs. It has been well said that ' the early
Christians . . . were infinitely more concerned about *God*, than
about themselves, far more preoccupied about doing His Will,
than given to speculating how much they received in the
Eucharist. . . . Communion, in short, was not *the* moment of
the early Eucharist; it was a corollary, an inevitable consequence
of God's will for man.'[2]

II

The act of receiving Communion reminds us of our absolute
dependence upon God. When we come to Communion we are
not only remembering something which God did once for all.
We know that Communion is a necessity, if we are to carry on
the work which Christ began, and continues through His Church.
The aim of Sacramental Communion is that we may continually
receive the love and power of God afresh, in order that we may
be able to give it out again to others.

Once more we are reminded of the life of Jesus upon earth.
As Man He lived in an attitude of complete dependence upon
God. He who was perfect Man was also fully God—yet in His
earthly life He depended entirely upon the Father for everything:
for all He had to do, or teach or suffer. Whether in the daily
rough-and-tumble of work at Nazareth, or in the responsibilities
and difficulties of family life, or in the solitude of the hills, when
He slipped away to pray, in all these conditions He lived with
unquestioning trust in God, with His eyes fixed upon God and
His will. His one prayer was : ' Father, glorify Thy Name.' So
in this mystery of Communion, through our membership in the
Body of Christ, we all receive something of the sacrificial life of
Jesus.

Let us go back once more to the *facts*. What did He *do* in that
Upper Room, on the ' night in which He was betrayed '?

First of all : *He broke bread*. It *had* to be broken. No loaf
can be eaten whole. So Christ *had* to die, He *had* to give His
Body to be broken before He could save us. The great Sayings of
Jesus about His Passion, which we read in the Gospels,[3] show
that He accepted His sufferings and His death as part of the

[2] F. Gavin, *Liturgy and Worship*, pp. 112-113.
[3] Mark 8.31; 10.33ff.; Luke 17.25, etc.

Purpose of God. He was convinced that—in the providence of God—'He must suffer'.

Then, *He gave the Bread to His friends*: thus showing that the great Act He was about to achieve—on the Cross—was *for them*. In the words of the Christmas carol: 'Christ was born to save'; but in order to save us He had to die. In the words of Dr. Forsyth: 'He was called and sent to die. He was born to die. It was in His blood. If He had not died, He would have lived an untrue life. . . . His mission was from God; and it was to be the Lover, Seeker, Saviour . . . of others, not of Himself. He gave Himself. . . . Doing, giving was the habitual natural bent and movement of His mind. He not only loved people, *He loved giving*. So He gave to all, not to a family few.'[4] And this giving was for all men. He gave the bread, He gave Himself, in order that we might all enter into our true relationship with God our Father.

And then: *He invited them to eat that Bread*: He asked them to *do* something—not merely to think, or to look, but to act, to *do*. The meaning of this symbolical action is profound; yet the simplest and most ignorant person knows what food means: something we cannot do without; if we have not enough to eat or if we cannot eat, we die. Food sustains our life; food helps us to grow. Food of the right kind protects us against disease. Food makes us strong. We need food adapted to our circumstances, all our life long. And so the symbolism of Food emphasizes our absolute dependence upon Christ, and the significance of the act of Communion.

The most illuminating and the most startling comment on this act of receiving bread and wine in Communion is the passage in the sixth chapter of John, where Jesus says: 'This is the Bread which cometh down from heaven, that a man may eat thereof, and not die.

'I am the Living Bread which came down from heaven: if any man eat of this Bread, he shall live for ever; and the bread that I will give is My Flesh, which I will give for the life of the world. . . . Then said Jesus unto them: Verily, verily, I say unto you, Except ye eat the flesh of the Son of Man, and drink His Blood, ye have no life in you. Whoso eateth My Flesh and drinketh My Blood, hath eternal life; and I will raise him up at the last day. For My Flesh is meat indeed, and My Blood is drink indeed.

[4] Forsyth, *The Church and the Sacraments*, p. 227.

'He that eateth My Flesh and drinketh My Blood, dwelleth in Me, and I in him.

'As the living Father hath sent Me, and I live by the Father: so he that eateth Me, even he shall live by Me.'

These words were as strange and startling to those who first heard them as they sound to-day. What do they mean?

'To eat the flesh' of Jesus means to receive the power which enabled Him, as Man, to give Himself to the utmost—even unto death. So we receive His Body in order that we may receive from Him His spirit of self-sacrifice, of self-giving to God and man. 'To drink the Blood' of Jesus means to receive His living power, the power of the Risen and Triumphant Lord—victor over sin and death—for in the Old Testament idea of sacrifice 'the blood is the life', and when the blood is shed the life is poured forth.

So in the act of Communion we receive Christ in all His living power. Through this Sacramental Communion He wills to dwell with us for ever. We are therefore to 'feed on Him in our hearts', and to abide in Him continually.

This 'feeding' on Christ means something which calls forth our utmost effort of response, although the act of reception is one of simple and tranquil faith. We know that we are utterly dependent upon Christ. We cannot serve, or pray, or suffer, or give ourselves, unless He communicates His power to us, and fills us with His Spirit of love and readiness for sacrifice. Yet in this intimacy of Communion He does give us a new energy, new power to endure, to suffer, to love and to give—to the uttermost, and to the end.

The history of the Church abounds in examples of this power at work in the lives of Christian men and women. In the early days we think of Ignatius of Antioch, a Bishop who was condemned to death in the year A.D. 107. On his long and painful journey to Rome, where he was to be thrown to the wild beasts in the Colosseum, he wrote Seven Letters which have been preserved. They show the spirit in which he faced suffering and death for the Faith of Christ. When he feared that some of his friends might try to arrange an escape (during the long journey) he wrote to protest against any such attempt. 'Allow me,' he writes, 'to be immolated while the altar is ready. . . . Let me be the prey of wild beasts; by them I shall attain to God. I am God's grain: let me be ground by the teeth of wild beasts, so that I may become the pure bread of Christ.' That was his desire, not merely to 'receive' but to 'become' the 'pure bread of Christ'.

During the ages of persecution the Eucharist, and readiness to 'drink the Cup' of Christ, were always closely associated. Cyprian, for instance, who died a martyr's death in A.D. 258, writes thus to his flock when he foresees troubles impending: 'We ought not to think that everything will go on as it has done hitherto; rather there awaits us a far harder and more terrible conflict, for which Christ's soldiers must prepare themselves with unshakable faith, and with much energy; they should therefore consider that for this reason they ought to drink the Cup of Christ *daily*, in order that they may be enabled to shed their blood for Christ.'

Speaking of the priest who officiates at the Eucharist, Cyprian says: 'Truly the priest stands there in Christ's stead, for he represents what Christ has done, and he brings a true and full sacrifice to God in the Church when he so celebrates as Christ Himself has plainly sacrificed Himself. . . . *We ought not to act otherwise than as Christ has acted.*'

This challenge comes afresh to the Church in every generation. In the seventeenth century, for instance, a French writer reminds us of this summons to 'act as Christ acted': 'He who often receives Christ in the Holy Communion and still shirks suffering, certainly does not communicate as he ought, because he does not receive the highest effects of the divine union, which is that we should be filled with the love which animated Jesus on earth.' He goes on to say that much prayer and frequent Communion does give people 'the courage of a lion', and enables them to act, to serve, and to suffer.

In a recent missionary exhibition there stood, alone, a small battered chalice: out of this Cup thousands of Malagasy Christians had received the wine of Communion before being hurled over a great cliff to their death, during a time of fierce persecution, in the nineteenth century.

III

Finally we come to the last of the six aspects of the Eucharist[5] which we have been considering: the *Mystery of the Presence*. In the act of Communion we 'know in Whom we have believed'; we know that we are in the Presence of our Living

[5] See Chapter I, p. 19.

Lord. Just as Christ made Himself known to His friends in the Breaking of Bread during the Forty Days after His resurrection: at a common meal, or on the seashore after a hard night of fruitless fishing, in the midst of daily life, so, all down the ages has He made Himself known to His people.

Here we are not dealing with theory but with fact. It is the universal experience of the Church throughout the world that Christ is present, in a special way, in the Sacrament. *How*—we do not know. We only know that *He is there*. Here Christ is One and undivided. Here He gives Himself to all who in simple faith and obedience obey His 'last and kindest word'.

In the Eastern Orthodox Church, 'the Eucharist', says a Russian Christian, 'is the vital nerve of the Church's life. To the faithful it is the most impressive and concrete realization of the promise "Lo I am with you always, even unto the end of the world". . . . The suffering Lord is also the Living, the Glorified and the Risen Lord, and the whole Eucharist is illumined by the radiance of His Resurrection.'[6]

St. Leonard, a member of the Franciscan Order, expresses the faith of his church when he says: 'O my soul, reflect seriously on the great truth of the Faith, which teaches thee that thy God is really present in the most holy Sacrament of the Eucharist. Thou hast here the same Saviour who was born in a stable, who died upon the Cross, who rose glorious and immortal from the dead, and is now seated at the right hand of His Father in heaven. . . . God is here . . . under the appearance of bread to become thy food. He, the Almighty, is ready to make His dwelling in thee. Prepare thyself then, my soul, to receive Him.'

And it is a German Lutheran who sings:

> *Not such brightness bringeth morning*
> *to the nightbound earth,*
> *Not such freshness, showers waking*
> *Flowers to new birth,*
> *As the life, the warmth, the sunlight*
> *Jesus brings to me,*
> *All renewing and refreshing*
> *With His Charity.*

Kierkegaard, the Danish Lutheran, the great philosopher and thinker, is full of the joy of Christ's Presence in the Sacrament.

[6] Arseniew, *Mysticism and the Eastern Church*, p. 131.

He constantly urges his hearers to believe that when they come to Communion 'He Himself is present; He blesses the Bread when it is broken; it is His blessing in the Chalice when it is handed to thee . . . at the altar *He* is the blessing'.

Again, a Free Church woman of the nineteenth century records in her *Journal*:

'At the Sacrament to-day I had the substance of the Feast, my very Christ, who is more precious than words can tell. . . . To-day He has been made known in the breaking of bread.'

Thus all down the ages, and in very different traditions, the 'faithful' bear witness to the 'Real Presence' of the Risen Lord in the Sacrament.

Here there is no room for speculation, or for rigid attempts to define the 'mystery of the Presence'. It is enough for us to know that Christ *is* present in the Eucharist; but at the same time we realize that He is not limited to this one method of manifestation. He gives Himself freely, to whom, and where He chooses. We know too much about the experience of those Christians who do not—for good reasons of their own—celebrate the Sacrament outwardly, to be aware that Christ does manifest Himself to those who worship Him in other ways. The early Quakers are an instance of this:

'The Lord of heaven and earth,' says Francis Howgill, 'we found to be at hand; and as we waited upon Him in pure silence His heavenly Presence appeared in our assemblies, when there was no language or speech from any creature.'[7] In all reverence we can only adore the freedom and the limitless generosity of His love.

A striking instance of such manifestation is very recent. Simone Weil (b. 1909), a French woman of Jewish birth and agnostic upbringing, was drawn towards the Christian Faith by many currents of thought and experience. In 1938 she spent Holy Week at Solesmes, attending all the services of the season. She gives her own description of this turning-point in her life:

'I was suffering all the time from acute headaches; every sound hurt me like a blow; but by an extreme effort of concentration I was able to leave this miserable body behind, to suffer alone in its corner, while I experienced pure joy in listening to the incomparable beauty of the chants, both words and music. This experience showed me how it is possible to love God in the midst of unhappiness. I need not add that in the course of this week

[7] Quoted by E. Underhill, *Worship*, p. 156.

the thought of the Passion of Christ entered into me profoundly, once for all.'

It was during this week that she met a young Englishman who was also staying near the Abbey. She saw him go forward to Communion and she saw him return from the altar. Never before had she seen such an expression of joy and peace in the face of anyone, and she was deeply impressed. In the course of conversation with him later on he told her of the metaphysical poets of the seventeenth century in England; she was a good English scholar, and when she went home she began to read some of this poetry. One day she came across George Herbert's poem: *Love Bade Me Welcome*.[8] She liked it so much that she learned it by heart. Often she would recite it to herself when her headache was almost unbearable, 'leaning', as she says, 'on the tenderness' it contained. 'I thought,' she said, 'that I was simply reciting a beautiful poem; but without knowing it, this poem had already become a prayer. It was during one of these recitations of the poem that Christ entered into my heart and took me captive for Himself.' She tells the friend to whom she was writing: 'In all my arguments about the problem of God, I had never even imagined the possibility of a human being coming into personal contact with God. . . . In this sudden experience of Christ, neither my senses nor my imagination were involved; I simply felt through my suffering the presence of a Love like that of a smile on the face of someone one loves.'[9]

Yet this supreme act of Communion, based as it is on the certainty of Christ's special Presence, is beyond and independent of thought and feeling. Unless this fact is realized, difficulties are bound to arise which will dim the certainty of faith, and check the free outpouring of desire and surrender.

Some people, of course, have believed in the Presence of Christ in the Sacrament all their lives—to such an extent that they take it for granted as a 'truth' which everyone accepts. Others—especially where the 'memorial' aspect of the Sacrament has been emphasized at the expense of the other aspects, may have failed to realize or even to believe in this glorious truth. Like short-sighted people who have never even seen the shapes of leaves till they were given the right glasses, such persons may go on for years dutifully receiving the Sacrament at stated times,

[8] See p. 39.
[9] Simone Weil, *Attente de Dieu*, pp. 20 and 76. Int. by the Rev. R. P. Perrin, O.P.

because it is the custom of the church, but without any real understanding of its meaning. And then perhaps a word, or a flash of vision lights up for a moment the meaning of the Eucharist, and the Lord's Presence is known in the Breaking of Bread.

The flash of vision passes; the insight is no longer vivid. But the effect remains. Never again can such a person go back to the previous state of blindness. We can never be sufficiently thankful for such gifts of grace. But in sacramental worship, as in every other part of the spiritual life, we have to walk by faith and not by sight. Here too, as in the life of prayer as a whole, we must learn to walk steadily along the safe path of an obscure faith.

So, whether we deplore the passing of a precious experience, or regret the fact that although we believe in the Real Presence of Christ in the Sacrament we 'cannot realize' it (as we say), we must come to terms with the fact that whatever moments of insight may have been granted to us now and again, it is more than possible to go to the Eucharist and to remain quite unmoved. Far from having any 'thrill' or emotion, we may indeed be full of the most tiresome distractions.

It is possible that such a state is due to some sin or carelessness which has not been faced, forgiven and put away. If we have been slack in prayer, inconsiderate to other people, uncharitable and unkind in speech or listening to, and retailing gossip, then naturally we shall feel out of place at the Eucharist. For the moment there is no contact between us and the God of Love and Mercy because *we* have closed the door. It is for us to re-open the door on our side by true repentance and confession, and the firm purpose to amend our lives.

Often, however, this sense of unreality persists, even when we have made the best preparation we can, and have tried to put our lives in order. What can we do about it? Is this haunting sense of unreality due to our own fault? Is something the matter with us? Such questions do arise, and must be faced.

There is always a danger that when these questionings arise in our hearts, and especially if we know no one to whom we can speak frankly about them, that we shall become worried, anxious and introspective. Then we may even become 'scrupulous', and wonder 'whether we ought to go to Communion when we feel like this?'

Others, without becoming either scrupulous or over-anxious,

are frankly perplexed. They even begin to have a faint wonder about the belief itself. 'Surely,' they say to themselves, 'the Real Presence ought to engender in us a real sense of itself: we ought in Communion, for instance, to be aware of something like a shock, a vibration, a repercussion in our very bodies of that almost unthinkable contact. . . . Yet we remain unimpressed.'

Such thoughts are very natural, but they are due to a misconception of the nature of the Sacrament and its purpose. Our life, says St. Paul, is 'hid' with Christ in God.[10] 'Thou art a God that hidest thyself.'[11] It is perfectly natural that God should hide His action from us and ask us to receive it in faith. Christ comes, it is true, but He wants to come to us quietly that we shall be natural with Him; He desires no formality. His 'Presence' is not that of a King granting an audience. His disguise is the disguise of love. He wants to come into our hearts as calmly and naturally as He passed through closed doors after His resurrection. So when He comes to us at the sacred moment of Communion, He comes very quietly, as quietly as the dawn. We open the door—He enters—and what He does we do not know; it is enough for us to know that He has come, and is there. 'We take His Presence with a simplicity which is a radiation from that Presence itself.'

So when we are thinking about the truth of the Presence of Christ in the Sacrament, would it not be better to put away, once for all, the often unspoken questions: Why should I go to the Sacrament? What shall I get out of it? Is it any use? Remembering that we come primarily as an act of obedience, shall we ask ourselves instead: Why does Christ come to us in this way? What is His Purpose? What does He want to do with us?

He comes because He desires us.

'With desire I have desired to eat this Passover with you . . .' He said to His friends at the Last Supper. It is as though He were saying to us all: '*You* knew nothing about it. *You* could not have imagined it! You will never understand it. I alone had this thought and this desire which I make a reality. I am here for you, because I want you for Myself.' He wants us, because He loves us.

He wants to lead us into His Friendship.

In Communion He comes to us as our Friend. The New Covenant in His Blood speaks louder than words, telling us that

[10] Col. 3.3.　　　　　　　[11] Isa. 45.15.

He is our Friend for evermore. So He comes to assure us that He is our Friend, who will never leave us, never forsake us.

He comes to make us strong.

He does not make us 'feel' strong; often we shall feel our sinfulness and weakness more acutely than ever. But He does make us strong: strong to work, to endure, to love, and hope, and pray, and give. He makes us strong enough to be single-minded, unselfish, generous to others, trustful towards God. He makes us strong to go on working without looking for any praise or appreciation from others, simply in order that we may please Him.

He comes to transform us.

He comes to make us like Himself. This is a very costing thing and He cannot do much with us unless we give Him a free hand. All He asks from us is an entire surrender, in docility and confidence. If we do not shrink from His saving and transforming action, He will do His creative and redeeming work in us, shaping us according to His will. So our constant prayer at every communion will be: 'Behold, the handmaid of the Lord, be it unto me according to Thy word.'

So the mystery of Communion is the 'mystery of consecration'. It is *God* who 'consecrates', yet we must bring our offering of an obedient love for Him to bless and use. As we yield ourselves into His hands to be treated as those who have in principle handed themselves over to Him, He will accomplish His will in us, by the free action of His grace. As Evelyn Underhill points out again and again in her writings, 'It is *God alone* who is the Mover, the Doer of all that is done. He alone uplifts, renews, transforms, converts, consecrates by the independent action of His grace; and this His consecrating action is mostly unperceived by us. His invisible rays beat upon, penetrate, and transform the soul. . . . The full power of those transforming rays could not be endured by us at all, if it rose to the level of consciousness, and was felt by sensitive natures.'[12]

The final word about this act of Communion is our utter dependence on God: trusting, calm, patient, knowing that we and the whole world are enfolded in a Love and a Mercy which knows all, understands all, and will always have the last word.

Thus 'the true consecrated life, however fully given to God, however deeply it may seem to be transformed, is never complete,

[12] E. Underhill, *The Mystery of Sacrifice*, p. 44.

rounded, self-supporting. On the contrary, it is a state of utter
and acknowledged dependence, a child-like life. And the more
the soul grows in love and self-abandonment, the more absolute
this dependence becomes.'[13]

IV

The early Liturgies are full of thanksgiving for the Sacrament.
In the Liturgy of Basil the Great, for instance, we read: *When
the Communion is ended, the Priest prays :* ' We give thanks to
Thee, O Lord our God, for the reception of Thy holy, spotless,
immortal, and heavenly mysteries, which Thou hast given us
for the benefit and sanctification and healing of our souls and
bodies.' Such prayers abound, suggesting, better than any specific
teaching could do, how instinctive is our response to the love of
God imparted in this life-giving Sacrament. At the present day,
and in the more sober language of the West, we too will naturally
want to make some act of thanksgiving before we leave the
church. The more simple we are about this the better; a few
words of our own, repeated quietly over and over again, will be
acceptable to God, especially when they are associated with the
firm resolve to follow Christ more closely at some point where
hitherto we may have failed. There will be days, however, when
our own words do not ' come '; then is the time to use the
language of the Church: either with a Psalm, or the *Te Deum*,
or a Communion Hymn, or the words of some classical prayer
which we have made our own.

At the same time, it is essential to remember that the Eucharist
is a social or corporate act; and the first part of our Thanksgiving
after Communion should be prayer with and for the whole
Church, as well as with and for the congregation or parish with
which we have been worshipping. Especially should we associate
our sacramental worship with the welfare of the whole Body of
Christ, giving thanks for all that is strong and hopeful at the
present day; and also offering our prayers for the restoration of
Christian unity throughout the world. We know that we are
already united in prayer and in faith, and our prayers and thanksgivings will be all the more fervent the more constantly we live
in the spirit of the ' given unity ' we already possess; and the more
earnestly we shall strive to make this ' given unity ' an outward
reality.

[13] E. Underhill, *The Mystery of Sacrifice*, p. 71.

No rules can be given for our more private thanksgivings. Chrysostom suggests that after Communion we should 'retire into a quiet place' and 'reflect attentively upon the great honour' that God has given us, in coming to us in Holy Communion. Sometimes our best prayer will be silence: the silence of love and confidence and repose. A great man of prayer once wrote: 'His Presence in this divine manifestation is most wonderfully marked by repose and silence. The Blessed Sacrament is the very centre of rest, the secret shrine of quietness. . . . Nowhere on earth do we feel so still and calm. . . . This should mark our life, for, as we receive our Lord, we receive Him in this same calmness. We are conformed to Him in proportion as our lives grow in quietness. . . . Even amid all that outwardly disturbs us, He is our Peace, sustaining our whole being.' For 'He so tempers His approach, so veils His Majesty, that the Divine Communion becomes the gentlest, the tenderest, the most perfectly restful hour of our life'.[14]

It is out of such quietness that courage is born. Our thanksgiving is an act of faith, an affirmation that we go forth in the strength of God to do His will, knowing that He has given Himself to us, and that He will give us all we need for every duty, every difficulty, every experience that we have to meet. Chrysostom says: 'We must go home from the Lord's Table like lions, breathing out fire, to put fear into the devil; considering in our hearts who is our Head, and what He has done for us out of love. . . .' For 'this Blood creates in us a royal beauty. . . . The nobility of the soul is increased and nourished thereby. . . . This Blood, when worthily received, drives the devil away. . . . This Blood, which has been poured out, cleanses the whole universe; it is the salvation of our soul, and by it our soul is washed clean, adorned and inflamed; it becomes brighter than fire, more radiant than gold. It has opened the way to heaven.'

Strengthen, O Lord, the hands which are stretched out to receive the Holy Thing; vouchsafe that they may daily bring forth fruit to Thy Divinity. . . . Grant that the ears which have heard the voice of Thy songs, may never hear the voice of clamour and dispute. Grant also that the eyes which have seen Thy great love, may also behold Thy blessed Hope; that the tongues which have sung the Sanctus may speak the truth.

LITURGY OF MALABAR

[14] Canon T. T. Carter.

O Lord our God, of boundless might, and incomprehensible glory, and measureless compassion, and ineffable love to man, look down, O Lord, according to thy tender love, on us, and on this holy house, and shew to us, and to them that pray with us, the riches of Thy mercies and compassion.

LITURGY OF ST. CHRYSOSTOM

The offered Christ is distributed among us. Alleluia!
He gives His body as food, and His Blood He pours out for us.
Alleluia!
Draw near to the Lord and be filled with His light. Alleluia!
Taste and see how sweet the Lord is. Alleluia!
Bless the Lord of heaven. Alleluia!
Bless Him in the highest heavens. Alleluia!
Bless Him all ye angels, bless Him all ye powers. Alleluia!

ARMENIAN LITURGY

O Thou my soul, bless God the Lord,
* and all that in me is,*
Be stirred up His Holy Name
* to magnify and bless.*

Bless, O my soul, the Lord thy God,
* and not forgetful be*
Of all His gracious benefits
* He hath bestowed on thee.*

PSALM 103

CHAPTER VIII

THE COMMUNICANT

How great a gift God offers us in this wonderful Sacrament of the Eucharist! Why then are so many members of the Christian Church indifferent to this gift? Why is it that so many people communicate rarely, or only on special occasions? Why is it that even regular 'Church-goers' often regard the Eucharist merely as 'another service'?

Probably there are several reasons for this indifference or laxity: ignorance of the meaning of the Sacrament, due either to lack of instruction, or to inattention and carelessness when right teaching has been given; or the cause may be moral: some sin unconfessed and unforgiven, some resentment nursed, some permanent bitterness of spirit allowed to poison the very springs of life—where any of these causes are present there can be no 'hearty desire' for the Sacrament, for the way is blocked.

But there are people who communicate regularly, as a matter of duty; indeed, they would be rather horrified if they failed to do so. Yet in their hearts they sometimes wonder why the Sacrament 'seems to do them so little good'. They are perplexed, and sometimes anxious and troubled about it; and they wonder where they 'have gone wrong'. If such people persevere in their effort to obey God in all things, in a spirit of humility and true repentance, they will not fail to receive the benefits of the Sacrament, though they may not always realize it.

But there are others, who also communicate from time to time, and are apparently sincere and devout, whose lives are nevertheless very imperfect, and sometimes even sub-Christian. It is not that they commit obvious or glaring sins, but rather that they are trivial, petty, and materialistic in their outlook on life. Often they are very 'touchy', inclined to brood over fancied slights; they are jealous and possessive in their personal relationships; in everyday life they are often irritable, impatient and disobliging. When their plans are upset they are easily annoyed and vent their irritation upon their families or their dependants. They are eager for praise and appreciation, and resent the least hint of criticism. They themselves, however, are usually very critical of others, and condemn them in no uncertain terms. Yet they read their Bibles, attend Church frequently, do 'Church work', subscribe to Missions—and are sure that they are very 'good Christians'. It is evident that such people lack self-knowledge; their religion is based largely on imagination and on feeling; prayer and life have become separated and to some extent both have 'gone bad'. Such people come to the Lord's Table with divided and distracted hearts. The failure is not in the Sacrament but in themselves. They need a fresh conversion.

The Eucharist is not magic. To be a real communicant involves a willing co-operation on one's own part. Various reasons may empty the practice of Holy Communion of all transforming power. Sometimes it is because people come to it with little sense of expectation; possibly it has become a mere matter of routine; there is no sense of wonder and no spirit of adoration. Others come rather rarely. They tend to associate 'Holy Communion' with 'the early service' which they occasionally take the trouble to attend before breakfast. But there is no great desire for the Sacrament, and no deep habit of worship. Some of course go further and abstain from frequent Communion on principle, lest familiarity should lead to formality. But in many instances the reason for failure to co-operate with the grace of God is due to lack of preparation; such preparation involves thought, and serious heart-searching, for there can be no real union with God while self is uppermost.

Thus the crux of the situation seems to lie with the communicant. The gift is there. The Church prepares the Table. The Sacrament is offered. 'Come, for all things are now ready,' says the Lutheran celebrant as he invites the congregation to come to the altar to receive the Sacrament. But unless there is due preparation, unless the whole personality is open to receive what God has to give, the effect will be slight. Serious thoughtful preparation is essential, if Christ is to have His way within us, and to transform us into His likeness. If we are free from deliberate and glaring sins such preparation need not be prolonged: 'Only be sure you bring with you faith and charity, clean hands, and a penitent heart.'[1]

[1] Jeremy Taylor, *The Golden Grove*, p. 92.

II

'Clean hands, and a penitent heart.' Clean hands? That is, putting right everything that we can put right by our own action: paying our bills, writing letters that are overdue, keeping our friendships in repair, making acts of restitution and of reconciliation which may cost a great deal. The resolute tackling of such urgent practical matters helps us to attack the more delicate and difficult matter of self-examination, recommended by St. Paul as part of our preparation for receiving the Sacrament. 'But let a man examine himself, and so let him eat of that bread and drink of that cup.'[2]

To some people these words sound mysterious and rather unreal. What need is there for all this 'fuss' about 'penitence'? they ask. The very idea of self-examination sounds strange, remote and rather morbid. Others are willing to admit that they have certain 'weaknesses', but they excuse themselves by saying 'It's my nerves!' or 'It's all due to my poor nerves!' or 'In my state of health what else can you expect?' Such excuses imply that we cannot help 'the way we are made', that we are in the grip of forces which are too strong for us.

The same attitude of semi-fatalism comes out in people who feel that the world of business or trade, or politics, is so 'impersonal' that they cannot be held responsible for practices which, in their hearts, they know to be wrong. As a rule persons of this kind live orderly private lives, and are often very pleasant and good-natured, but they are not prepared to admit that they are 'sinners'. They see no need for repentance. Others again do not consciously avoid self-examination, but they are very busy with social service; they serve on so many committees and do so many 'good works' that, as they say, 'they have no time to think about themselves'. Even their church-going is part of a ceaseless round of well-meaning activities. Clearly, such people will not undertake the serious effort of self-examination unless some searching or unusual experience arouses them to the reality of their situation.

Some people, however, if they do not actually avoid penitence, do all they can to tone it down, or to explain away their real sins. It is plain that the cause of all these excuses is pride and vanity. Dr. Inge was certainly not far out when he remarked that the

[2] I Cor. 11.28.

'straight and narrow way is never likely to be uncomfortably crowded'!

There are others, however, who sincerely want to lead a Christian life, and are conscious that all is not well with them. They are aware of failure, and they have a deep hidden desire for God. But they do not know where to begin. To such people, the wise practice of self-examination, leading to real penitence and faith, will be their best preparation for the regular practice of Communion.

III

The Sacrament will never mean anything to us unless we are willing to admit that we are sinners. This is a truth which most people hate. 'The final sin of man,' said Luther, 'is his unwillingness to admit that he is a sinner.' Sin is pride. Sin is rebellion—against God. The very human and general desire to be 'top-dog', to lord it over other people, to dominate, is simply an arrogant contempt for others, though it may be concealed under the plea that 'It is all for their good'. The desire for power, for recognition, for praise, the hatred of truth, the absence of humility, are all signs of the fundamental sin of pride. 'Pride,' says St. Augustine, 'is the beginning of all sin,' and Pascal exclaims: 'This "I" is hateful . . . it is essentially unjust, in that it makes self the centre of everything.' This sin comes out in many forms: as pride of power, as greed, or as pride of knowledge; above all, it appears as self-righteousness or spiritual pride, the worst and most terrible sin of all, and the most difficult to eradicate.

What kind of self-examination then, is required of these who wish to make serious preparation for Communion?

At a University Mission in Oxford, in 1931, Archbishop Temple said: 'There are many aids to self-examination. Some of them are excellent, but some are quite dreadfully bad.' He explained what he meant by saying: 'If they confront you with a series of questions, all referring to *actions*, they are bad, because our self-examination must not refer mainly to actions. . . . However searchingly these are treated the result will be, with regard to a large number of questions you will say "not guilty". And most times with regard to the ones that remain either you will decide that they do not matter very much, or else you will think that they do when they do not.'

The aim of self-examination is to gain the right kind of self-knowledge; but our preparation for the Sacrament has no self-regarding aim. Its purpose is to clear our hearts and consciences of everything that prevents Christ from entering fully into our hearts and lives. So the right kind of self-examination goes much farther than the 'discovery of sins'. What we really need to know is *ourselves*, for it is lack of this knowledge which works such havoc in people's lives. So many well-meaning persons are incredibly ignorant of themselves. They want to help others, and they try to do it, yet too often they blunder and tread on people's toes, to such an extent that people will do anything to get out of their way! It is pathetic and sometimes tragic to see how lonely these well-meaning ignorant persons are. In a family such people are difficult enough, but when they are given responsible positions in Church and State, in business or school or office, their ignorance and tactlessness often spoil their other good qualities. Self-examination of the right kind, that is, one that brings us gradually face to face with truth—the truth about ourselves—is the only way in which we can become the persons God wants us to be. Christ is the Truth, and in 'His light we shall see light'.

So with the sincere desire to face the Truth we need to find some way of examining ourselves that will help us on to the right lines. Probably most of us will find that it is wise to vary our methods; what suits us at one time will not continue to suit us all our life long. Here too we must be receptive and teachable, ready to move on, as life moves on.

Some people find that the plain and simple method of a list of questions based on the Ten Commandments meets their need; if these questions interpret the Commandments in the light of the New Testament, such examination can be both searching and salutary. Here is an example from the writings of a scholar and a theologian. Commenting on the first two Commandments, he says: 'Life for many of us slips by so smoothly, its wheels oiled with the quiet engrossment in this or that pursuit. . . . And sometimes, when we think about ourselves, it is a shock to find how very small a part we have allowed the thought of God to play in our lives. "None other Gods but ME . . . Him only shalt thou serve." And over and over again have come times when we are constrained to confess: "I have had none other gods but *me*, myself only have I served."' Then he goes on: 'I have sometimes tried, without praying about it, to do a piece of work that required divine wisdom or control, or held a conversation with a difficult person, or with a person in difficulty. I have sometimes passed a whole day or more without any prayer at all, as if I were self-sufficient. If I have received praise or thanks . . . there have been times when I accepted it for myself, as if it were mine, instead of handing it on at once as an offering to God, who alone enables me to do or be anything. I have thought about myself and admired myself; I have felt twinges of jealousy when I have heard other people admired. I have shirked or done badly things that involved taking trouble for others, or things that were not likely to show . . . and so on. Everyone knows for himself the ways in which he is tempted to self-centredness, self-worship.'[3] This is an honest and searching act of self-examination, in the light of the First Commandment.

Speaking of the Second Commandment, Dr. McNeile says: ' It makes us think of the dangers which beset us when we are engaging in religious acts in common worship, or our private prayers. . . . Very often we don't worship God at all. . . . Every time that our worship is insincere and unreal, formal and lifeless, every time that we confess our sins merely as a religious practice without being really sorry for them, every time that we receive the Body and Blood of the Lord with a sin on our conscience which we have not the firm and eager intention of trying to conquer, the inheritance is defiled. . . . From all self-worship, self-centredness or complacency, from all deadness and insincerity in prayer, and from unrepented sin—Good Lord, deliver us.'[4]

Another method is to examine oneself in the light of the Seven Capital Sins: Pride, Envy, Anger, Covetousness, Gluttony, Lust and Sloth. These sins are the root forms of *sin*: to make a distinction between them helps us to get down to *sin* itself and to see how deeply it is ingrained in our nature. To be aware of the presence of one of these ' capital sins ' in oneself is to be convicted of *sin*—to know that I am a sinner. It is only too true that these sins—in different forms—are as deeply rooted in religious people as in those who make no profession of the Christian faith. No one has pointed this out more plainly or with greater psychological penetration than St. John of the Cross.

Self-examination, however, if it is to be profitable, should not

[3] McNeile, *Devotion and Discipleship*, p. 246.   [4] Ibid., pp. 247-248.

dwell too much on the negative side. There is indeed a danger
that too much introspection may make preparation for the Sacrament a purely self-regarding affair, and thus defeat its own
object. The tendency to brood over our faults and failures
may lead us to forget our Lord, and thus to compare ourselves
with other people and not with Him. 'The only way to know
ourselves better is to know Christ better, and to be constantly
comparing ourselves not with other people but with Him.'[5] To
this end some positive methods of self-examination, based on the
New Testament, will be of great value.

For instance, we might take the *Hymn in Praise of Love* in
I Corinthians 13.1-8, reading it either in the original or in a
modern English version. Verse by verse, clause by clause, we
set to work to test our daily behaviour and our thoughts and
feeling by this Christ-like standard. Such an 'exercise' cannot
fail to be searching and fruitful, the more definitely we apply
it to our relations with the people with whom we are in most
constant contact.

Again, the whole of the *Sermon on the Mount* (Matthew,
Chapters 5, 6 and 7) will provide endless material for self-
examination. To begin with we could take the Beatitudes
(5.1-12). These sayings of Christ are a kind of mirror reflecting
the character and spirit of Jesus. If we expose ourselves to this
merciful yet searching light, we shall see our own sin more
clearly than ever before.[6]

Another valuable method is to take the *Lord's Prayer*, clause
by clause, thinking over each one carefully, and then asking ourselves: 'Do I really believe this?' and then 'Am I trying to live
according to this standard?'

At certain seasons it would be good to take *The Seven Words
from the Cross*; think and pray over them, and then apply what
we have learned to ourselves.

In a recent book[7] the writer says that whatever we may feel
about the necessity for self-examination, and however distasteful
or difficult the whole idea may seem, there is only one answer
to our queries: 'Look to Christ and let *Him* judge your condition.' 'We start from our Lord. It is He who is to judge us
and not we ourselves.'

Self-examination, however, is not an end in itself. We are to

[5] McNeile, *Devotion and Discipleship*, p. 407.
[6] See pp. 124ff. for an expansion of this method.
[7] M. Jarrett Kerr, *Our Trespasses*, p. 85.

examine ourselves in order that we may repent of our sins. What then do we mean by 'repentance' or 'penitence'?

If our self-examination has been thorough and honest we shall be painfully aware that sin is not 'weakness' but 'rebellion'. We know that we have sinned against *God*; that we have followed our own will rather than His; that we have sought our own way and our own glory rather than His; in a word, that we have been turning away from God to please ourselves. Further, we shall see that there is all the difference between sin and vice. We may be extremely virtuous and have the highest ideals; we may live lives that are outwardly correct and even 'religious', and yet we may be 'law-breakers', because every day and hour we break the Law of Love. It is only in the light of Christ that we see how sinful we are, that we see our indifference to others, our bad temper, our hateful uncharitableness and spiteful gossip, for what it really is, sin against God, who is Holy Love. It is these sins, so often committed, so lightly esteemed, which separate us from God.

Thus we need repentance both at the outset of the Christian life and all our life long. Indeed, the nearer we come to God the more clearly do we perceive our sins. It was the great Saint Teresa, who knew so much of God, who died with the cry of penitence upon her lips: 'Create in me a clean heart, O God.'

Thus penitence is the act by which we return from a state of rebellion against the will of God to a state of obedience. For the Christian, sin is more than a moral failure; it is unfaithfulness to our Friend and our Lord. When we realize this we become deeply 'sorry'. But we must not be too much troubled if we do not always *feel* sorry. If we are determined, as far as possible, to avoid all occasions of sin, and with the help of God to resist temptation, then we are penitent, whatever we may feel. Such penitence is real, though it is far from perfect.

When we have tried to discover our sins, in the light of Christ, and have acknowledged them, in plain words, either to ourselves, or to some other person, we then proceed to confess them to God. This means making a definite *act of repentance*. However brief it may be, this should be the climax of the process of self-examination, and as definite as possible. We then *take* forgiveness. This is an act: an act of acceptance, grateful, believing and humble. It is this 'definiteness' which clears the air, and makes our prayers for forgiveness real, and sends us out released from haunting thoughts and fears and anxieties. For 'God forgives us, not because of what we are, but because of what *He* is'. So long as we are trying to do the will of God, even if we know we do it very imperfectly and are constantly falling away from even our own idea of what we ought to be, we must never allow any hesitation or uncertainty to follow our acts of confession and penitence. *God forgives us not only for what we have done but for what we are.* And when He forgives, He does it royally and freely, and He wills that we should be at peace. For 'He who has travelled so far to find us, will not refuse us when we are found; and to be received by that Love is to be saved'.

IV

Preparation for the Eucharist is necessary. We need to make a real effort to overcome distraction, to 'recollect' ourselves, and to set our minds and wills in order before God. And all this involves, as we have seen, a very real act of repentance, coupled with practical acts of reconciliation and restitution. But when this has been done it is essential that we should turn our eyes away from ourselves, and our sins and failings, towards God Himself. True penitence indeed is often given more fully to those who expose themselves to the tender mercy of our God, than to those who spend too long in anxious self-absorbed introspection.

A great part of our special preparation therefore should be given to grateful, loving, adoring reflection upon the love of God, who has given us this Sacrament as a visible pledge and assurance of His undying love. God's love is always generous, free, and forgiving; He is always seeking us with tender love, in patience and gentleness and persistence. And in the Eucharist God draws us to Himself in a very personal way.

All down the ages men and women have found the love of God in this 'rich Sacrament', and this not in a vague, general way, but focused as it were by a burning glass upon each individual personally. Here are two testimonies, very far apart in time and in outlook, yet they are one in their adoring gratitude for the love of Christ made known to us in the Eucharist.

The first witness is an Italian woman, a follower of St. Francis in the Middle Ages: the Blessed Angela of Foligno. After a sinful and mis-spent youth she was 'soundly converted' to Christ. She then retired—as soon as she was free to do so—from the world, and lived very quietly as a Franciscan Tertiary with one like-minded companion near Foligno in the lovely Vale of Spoleto. There she gave herself to prayer and the instruction of a group of disciples. Speaking of the Sacrament she says:

'This Sacrament is above all things gracious and kindleth love. For that which moveth Him who ordained this most Holy Sacrament was the greatest of all things. . . . I know not what name I should give it, save that of immeasurable love, because of His boundless love did He institute this Sacrament. Because of His great love towards us did He enter into the Sacrament and will abide therein to the end of the world. This he did not only in memory of His Death, but that He might ever and always remain nigh unto us.' 'O burning and unquenchable love! Such was and is the love which He bare unto us!' 'What soul is there . . . who, profoundly reflecting on that love, would not feel moved to return the love of such a Lover, who never forgot us, either in life or in death, but did wholly give Himself that He might be for ever united with us in love.'[8]

Such words carry their own conviction; they are as living now as when they were first written in the thirteenth century. Yet the trouble with so many of us is that we do not think often enough, or deeply enough about the reality of the love of God; indeed, unconsciously, we are often harbouring hard thoughts of God, and thus setting up a barrier between us and Himself. Baxter, the great Puritan divine, writes feelingly about this. He says:

'Ever keep thy soul possessed with believing thoughts of the infinite love of God. . . . No doubt it is the death of our heavenly life to have hard thoughts of God. . . . O! that we could always think of God as we do of a friend, as of one that unfeignedly loves us, even more than we do ourselves; whose very heart is set upon us to do us good. . . . I fear most Christians think higher of the love of a hearty friend than of the love of God!'[9] And nowhere are we confronted more tenderly and more urgently with the love of God than in the Sacrament of His Love.

From an Italian woman of the thirteenth century we now turn to the Danish thinker of the nineteenth century—the famous 'melancholy Dane', Søren Kierkegaard. Towards the close of his strangely tormented life Kierkegaard experienced a great

---

[8] *The Book of Divine Consolation of the Blessed Angela of Foligno*, pp. 148-149.
[9] *The Saints' Everlasting Rest*.

spiritual liberation—through the forgiveness of sins, which came home to him with greater power than ever before, and transformed his life. This experience is reflected frequently in his later books, and especially in the addresses for Communion which he gave in a church at Copenhagen.

Speaking of this 'hearty desire' for the Sacrament he says:

'I heartily long for this Supper, for this Supper which is remembrance of Him. . . . Longing for fellowship with thy Saviour and Redeemer is precisely the thing which should increase with every occasion of remembering Him. He is not dead but living. . . . He indeed is to be and to become thy life. . . . And therefore as hearty longing belongs to a worthy remembrance of Him, so again it belongs to a hearty longing that it increases with remembrance. . . .'[10]

'He was betrayed—but He was Love: *in the night in which He was betrayed* He instituted the Supper of Love! Always the same! For those that crucified Him He prayed; and in the night in which He was betrayed He utilized the opportunity (Oh! infinite depth of love . . .) to institute the Supper of reconciliation. . . . Behold, everything is now ready . . . He is waiting here at His Holy Table.'[11] Again, speaking on the words *Love hides the multitude of sins*, he says, 'He dies once for the sins of the whole world and for thy sins; His *death* is not repeated, but *this* is repeated; that He died also *for thee*, for thee who dost receive the pledge that He died *also for thee*, this is repeated at the altar where He gives *Himself* to thee for a shelter. . . . He gives thee Himself as a shelter; it is not some comforting thought He gives thee, it is not a doctrine He communicates to thee; no, He gives thee Himself. . . .'[12]

The way in which we make these meditations on the love of God will depend upon our usual habits of prayer. God leads us by many ways, and what helps one person may mean little or nothing to another. But if we take our preparation seriously we shall know what to do. Speaking generally, it seems obvious that such meditation should always include some slow and careful reading of the story of the Passion, in the Gospels. Sometimes it is good to read the whole story at a sitting, in one Gospel. At other times we can take one incident or one phrase or one verse of the Passion Story and let that sink into us and thus enfold us in the Love of God in Christ.

[10] *Christian Discourses*, p. 268.   [11] Ibid., p. 288.
[12] *For Self Examination*, p. 23.

For love God came to man, and God became man; for love, God being invisible, became like His servants. For love, He was wounded for our sins, and in those wounds of our Saviour is the safe and quiet rest of us weaklings and sinners. . . . The wounds of Jesus Christ are full of mercy, full of pity, full of sweetness, and full of love.

Cleanse us, O Lord, from our secret faults, and mercifully absolve us from our presumptuous sins, that we may receive Thy holy things with a pure mind; through Jesus Christ our Lord.

O Lord our God, Father, Son, and Holy Spirit, make us ever to seek and love Thee, and by this Holy Communion which we have received never to depart from Thee; for Thou art God, and beside Thee there is none else, for ever and ever. Amen.

CHAPTER IX

THE EUCHARIST IN THE WORLD CHURCH

F ROM his cell in a German prison in the year 1937, a Lutheran pastor wrote to a friend: 'The book on "Fellowship in the Eucharist" is giving me much joy. . . . Perhaps in our Church we are now experiencing something of what Traugott Hahn discovered in a time of persecution in his contact with Bishop Tychon of the Greek Orthodox Church: *unitas in differentia*; our union in confessing Jesus Christ, the One Lord of the Church.'[1]

This experience of oneness in the Eucharist, and of the centrality of the Eucharist, has been frequently repeated in the most recent history of the Church. A young pastor of the French Reformed Church, speaking of the movements of renewal in his own land, said to the writer: 'Wherever there is new life in our church, there is always renewed emphasis on three things: Prayer, the Bible, and the Eucharist . . . and the three go together.' In this book we are thinking of the centrality of the Eucharist, as one strand in this threefold cord, on which the life of the Church depends.

I

· Not only in past ages, but at the present time, wherever the 'Holy Church throughout all the world' has taken root, there the 'altar fire' of the Eucharist has been lit. In the great island of New Guinea, for instance, an Anglican Mission began work, in 1891, among cannibals and head-hunters. On August 10th, 1941, this diocese celebrated its Jubilee with great rejoicing. At 7 a.m. a great congregation gathered in the Cathedral: the

[1] *Und lobten Gott*, p. 47.

Bishop and an English priest, assisted by two Papuan clergy, conducted the service. The English Bishop wrote afterwards: 'The Jubilee Day itself was indeed a "golden day" . . . The Eucharist at 7 a.m. . . . with Papuan clergy . . . doing everything with the utmost reverence and perfection . . . was one of those services that one feels is too sacred even to attempt to describe. It was as if Heaven had been brought down to earth. The Cathedral was crowded to the doors, and the quiet reverent atmosphere of devotion was something we can never forget. There were over eight hundred communicants, and as I was taking part in the administration, the realization of what it all meant was something overwhelming; that fifty years ago the Name of our Saviour was unknown to the people in these parts of Papua, until the pioneers landed in the early morning of that day, and yet now here was an almost unending stream of devout and reverent communicants coming up to kneel at the Altar, that they might be united to Him in His Most Holy Sacrament. Fifty years ago they did not know Him, but indeed they know Him now!'[2]

Six months later war flared up in Papua. The Anglican missionaries decided to stay at their posts, knowing what this might mean; one of them, Vivian Redlich—a young man—'was about to celebrate Holy Communion with his native people when word was brought to him that he was to be seized by the Japanese. He spent a moment or two in silent prayer and then said: "It is the Lord's Day, and the Lord's service that I am taking, and I intend to see it through." And he did.'[3] Immediately afterwards he and several others were betrayed by non-Christian Papuans and killed by the Japanese.

All over Europe, during the war years, in circumstances of extreme difficulty and danger, the Eucharist was often celebrated by priests in hiding or in disguise: sometimes in frozen dugouts in the depths of the forest, close to Red Army sentries, patrolling near at hand; sometimes in prison cells or sick-rooms, or in poor lodging houses, and often at 1 a.m. as the safest hour.

Bishop Sloskans, a Latvian by birth, who had entered Russia secretly, in order to help to maintain the life of his Church there during an era of severe persecution, was captured by the Russian Secret Police, and tortured so severely that when he was only in his thirties he looked like an aged broken man. He spent seven

[2] *South Sea Epic*, pp. 13-14. (S.P.G.)   [3] Ibid., p. 68.

years in imprisonment in Siberia and on the shores of the White Sea. In some way or another it became known that this prisoner was a Bishop, and one political prisoner after another managed to provide grapes and bread for the Sacrament. Secretly and at night he celebrated the Eucharist, and gave Communion to over one thousand Catholics in the Siberian Camp till he was most marvellously set free.[4]

In Russia during a period of persecution there were many 'secret priests'[5]—men who wore ordinary clothes, did ordinary work, and yet managed to carry on the worship of the Church 'underground'. Under such conditions the central act of Christian worship becomes a capital crime against the State. Yet so deep is the desire for the Sacrament that men and women will risk their lives to take Communion.

These instances come from Eastern Europe and from the Roman Catholic and Eastern Orthodox Churches. Now let us turn to the West, and to the Protestant Churches. Bishop Lilje's experience in prison on Christmas Eve, 1944, ranks high among these great Sacramental occasions. Dr. Lilje had been in prison since August of the previous year, and his fate was still uncertain; he never knew whether at any moment he would be wakened in the middle of the night to be taken away and shot. On this Christmas Eve he was alone in his cell, thinking of his family and his congregation, and longing to be allowed to exercise his ministry, when his number was called; a guard came to the door and told him to follow. Wondering what was about to happen, Lilje obeyed. He was taken to the Commandant, who led the way silently to another cell. At the door of this cell the Commandant stood still, and said to the guard, 'Bring No. 212 here too!' Then he went into the cell, taking the Bishop with him. As they entered, a man rose to his feet whom Dr. Lilje at once recognized as a certain Count X; he greeted him with eager friendliness, but the Commandant broke in roughly upon their conversation: 'I did not bring you two gentlemen together for social purposes.' Turning to the Count he said, 'You asked for a pastoral visit from a Chaplain who is your friend; unfortunately this was not possible, but here is Dr. Lilje, who will speak to you.' Dr. Lilje then asked the Count what he would like him to do. He replied: 'I would like to make my confession and receive the Sacrament.' A cup was provided, a small amount of

[4] 'Father George', *Through God's Underground*, p. 126.
[5] i.e., of the Orthodox Church.

wine, and some white bread. Meanwhile No. 212 was brought in; he was an accomplished violinist. The service began with a beautiful Christmas chorale played by the musician. Then Bishop Lilje proceeded to celebrate the Eucharist according to the Lutheran custom; as the Count knelt on the stone floor to receive absolution and Communion the tears ran down his face, but it was a peaceful hour, full of the Presence of Christ; the Commandant himself was deeply moved; when the service was over he shook the Bishop's hand with great warmth, saying: 'I thank you. You do not know what you have done for me this evening in the midst of my difficult heart-breaking work.' With joy and praise in his heart the Bishop was taken back to his cell. Later he heard that Count X was soon removed to a concentration camp; the violinist was murdered by the Gestapo; and the Commandant was relieved of his post because he was too humane. But the memory of that Christmas celebration in 1944 has remained a precious memory with Bishop Lilje ever since.

Pastor Niemöller, who spent so many years in prison for conscience sake, had some great experiences in common worship in the concentration camp at Dachau, especially during the last part of the War from 1944 to 1945. Later he published *Six Dachau Sermons* which were preached during this period. There were at first only six persons present at these services: Dutch, Norwegian, English, Jugoslav and Macedonian—and Niemöller himself: German; later this congregation was joined by two more Germans, a man and wife. These people belonged to many different churches: Calvinist (or Presbyterian), Lutheran, Anglican, and Eastern Orthodox. All of them were completely cut off from all church life as well as from their families and their friends.

'What then could we do?' says Niemöller in his Preface to the book, 'save to put the "*una Sancta*" into practice and to gather together to hear and receive the Word of God? And indeed what else could we do also than to celebrate the Lord's Supper together?' . . . At any rate, that's what we did, and all our hearts were gladdened and refreshed by the fellowship which united us as the disciples of one Master and One Saviour.'

This 'ecumenical' congregation met in an ordinary cell (No. 34), which was also used as a chapel by three Roman Catholic priests with whom Niemöller was imprisoned. It contained a very simple altar—a table with a crucifix and candles. To this small congregation Niemöller spoke very beautifully and simply about the meaning of the Lord's Supper, closing his sermon with these words:

'To the great community of those who on this evening proclaim the Lord's Death as "Good News" we too belong; we who are here coming to this table: a small company, each of us forcibly separated from home and loved ones, all of us deprived of our freedom, all of us in uncertainty, not knowing what the coming day—or hour—will bring forth! We eat and drink at our Father's Table, and we may be of good courage: there is no longer anything to separate us from Him, since our Lord and Master has given Himself for us, and for many. . . .'

Prisoners of war, too, were greatly helped by the Sacrament in the weary years of captivity. Here is one instance, from a German source. The incident is headed:

The Sacrament Under the Pear Tree. 'Together with our Catholic comrades we had made an altar, whose sole ornament was a Cross covered with tin, which shone and glittered in the sunshine. We usually placed this altar under the shade of a large and ancient pear tree. It was the only tree in the camp which the men who were looking for firewood had left untouched. Even if we had a sudden shower quite a large number of men could shelter under this tree and keep dry. That was our "Church Under the Pear Tree". There at the beginning of June we celebrated the Eucharist. We had waited till evening to allow the noise of men's voices to die down gradually; an hour before the appointed time a sudden thunder-storm swept over the place and made us wonder whether we could hold the service after all. But very soon a warm summer wind sprang up and dried everything, to our great delight, so that we were able to come together as arranged. There were about two hundred Communicants. We had a bottle of red wine, and a loaf of white bread for the elements. Our ciborium, paten and jug had been made out of old tins. They shone in the evening sunshine as though they were vessels of gold. For a chalice we had an ordinary glass. All the men had tidied themselves as best they could and the whole service was full of a deep earnestness.' All through their time of imprisonment these men found their greatest comfort in the Eucharist.

II

It is not only in times of distress and danger that the Eucharist is known to be the very heart of the life of the Church. All over the world, wherever the Christian Faith is established, the Eucharist is the central act of worship, and 'daily bread' to the faithful worshipper. Forms of worship vary greatly. What is precious and significant in the West may often seem meaningless or dull to Christians in Asia or Africa. But every race finds the Sacrament to be both its greatest treasure and its highest opportunity. It is indeed the universal and supreme act of the worship of the Church.

In countries where the Church is young, very often something of the freshness of the Primitive Church is expressed. For instance, in many churches in the West there is a widespread tendency to regard the Eucharist as 'something extra' especially for 'pious people'. It has become too much a matter for the individual. But in new Christian communities the corporate sense has been emphasized from the first. An experienced missionary writes: 'It is possible that the churches which have been gathered from the races of India and Africa may redress the balance by recalling the Church of the West to this essential aspect of eucharistic worship. The monthly Eucharists in Chota Nagpur, at which the faithful from scattered villages assemble together for the purpose of taking their part in offering the one oblation, approach far more nearly to the Sunday worship of the Primitive Church than anything I know in the West.'[6]

When we think of the extent of the world-wide Church, and picture small groups of Christians gathering together to celebrate the 'Lord's Death till He come', we gain a great sense of family unity. Here are some pictures of the Church at worship throughout the world.

In Burma an English missionary lives in a jungle village 'at the back of beyond'. He has an outpost fifteen miles away, in the charge of two Christian Karens; there is one other Christian in the village. These men are surrounded by heathen and militant Buddhists. Once a month these three men gather in Christ's Name in a poor hut which seems ready to tumble down at every gust of wind and rain. There Christ comes to His own in the

[6] H. P. Thompson, *Worship In Other Lands*, p. 162. (S.P.G.)

Sacrament, and their faces show what they could never put into words.

Now we turn to the region of Arctic snows. At one place a number of Christian Eskimo have asked the missionary to celebrate the Eucharist; when he arrived they had made ready for him in the only possible place—one of their snow huts. He gives a vivid description of the service in its Eskimo setting. 'First they cleared the place of all rotten meat, etc., and then fresh snow, white and clean, was brought in. A tent was arranged (under the snow roof) to catch any drops that might fall when the hut was crowded during the service. The floor was then covered with caribou skins, so that the worshippers might kneel with less discomfort. A sledge box was placed in a central position on the sleeping platform and acted as the Holy Table, and when carefully covered with new towels of spotless white the sacramental linen and vessels were arranged upon it. Two flickering stone lamps shed a subdued light hardly sufficient for reading, but not unsuitable for the service. The communicants were ten in number, four women and six men. . . . It is no exaggeration to say that, in an almost literal manner, the experience of the disciples who walked to Emmaus was repeated at this time, and the Lord was made known to His disciples in the breaking of bread. . . . After the service the people did not go away. For nearly ten minutes no words were spoken. It was as if we all with one accord felt in our souls that it was "good for us to be here", for we had seen the Lord.'[7]

A third picture comes from the forests of Borneo. The setting is a long Dyak house, in which some thirty-six families are living under one roof. The building is raised on posts about eight feet from the ground; the house has a number of living-rooms and a large common verandah; a corridor runs right through the house and is a public way. Inside there is a confused medley of children, dogs and fowls; below the house are grunting and squealing pigs; there is an indescribable din. In this noisy place there is only one Christian family; the English missionary comes to give Communion to this isolated group. 'Next morning he prepares for the service in the tiny room. Round the walls are cockerels in cages, crowing with might and main; but the Dyaks are used to the noise and are not disturbed by it. Through every chink and cranny in the walls peer inquisitive eyes. Amid such surroundings the Lord's own service is held, and for a brief

[7] H. P. Thompson, *Worship In Other Lands*, p. 165. (S.P.G.)

while other things are almost forgotten. The two or three are gathered in His Name; and He who was born in a stable will not despise the lowly habitation of those He came to save.'[8]

Thus all over the world, under all kinds of conditions, in exile, prison, concentration camp, on the brink of death, as well as in the midst of daily life and at times of festival and rejoicing, the Eucharist is the Feast of the whole Christian Family: 'in heaven and on earth'. And wherever it is celebrated we are 'at home', for here is the foretaste of the Father's House which is for all nations.

[8] H. P. Thompson, *Worship In Other Lands*, p. 166.

'UNTIL HE COME'

In the Eucharist the Church perpetually reconstitutes the crisis in which the Kingdom of God came in history. It never gets beyond this. At each Eucharist we are there—in the night in which He was betrayed, at Golgotha, before the empty tomb on Easter Day, and in the Upper Room where He appeared; and we are at the moment of His coming, with angels and archangels and all the company of heaven, in the twinkling of an eye, at the last trump. Sacramental communion is not a purely mystical experience, to which history would be in the last resort irrelevant; it is bound up with a corporate memory of real events.

C. H. DODD

It is not man alone who is affected by the redemption and the joy of victory; with the joy over our resurrection is linked also the joy over the redemption of the whole world, over the ending of the dominion of corruption, over the redemption of all creation and the dawn of the kingdom of life. And the eye of the spirit gazes fervently out towards the glory to come—that splendid 'freedom of the children of God', of which all creation shall partake. The Resurrection is thus an event of cosmic significance, and the world, equally with man, is thereby already permeated by the radiance of the celestial glory, although as yet in hidden form, and has attained to a new and high worth; for it has already taken into itself the germ of immortality. Christ, so sings the Eastern Church, is 'risen as God from the grave in glory and hath thereby raised the whole world with Him. . . . Therefore is the whole world, the whole creation, summoned to rejoice and sing praises to the Lord. . . .'

ARSENIEW, *Mysticism and the Eastern Church*, p. 35

AT every Eucharist the Church looks back, to Christ's Death
and Resurrection; at every celebration she knows Him to be
present, Risen, Ascended, her Great High Priest, her Living
Lord; and at every celebration she looks forward to His final
Coming, when the Kingdom of God will come with power.
This sense of past, present, and future, focused in one supreme
act of worship, was very strong in the Early Church. The last
book in the New Testament, the Book of Revelation, is full of
allusions to the worship of the Church: in mysterious imagery
the writer evokes the reverence and awe and the exultant joy of
the Early Church at worship, as she bows before the One Eternal
God ' which was, and is, and is to come ', whose purpose will be
perfectly fulfilled in Christ, her Exalted Lord.

The earliest liturgical prayer is *Marana tha*: ' Our Lord,
Come! '[1] Evidently it was offered at the Eucharist with a two-
fold meaning: first of all, it was a prayer to the Risen Lord, asking Him to ' come ' to His assembled People; and, secondly, it
was a prayer for the coming of Christ in judgment and in
victory, an act of faith in the Sovereignty of God. The New
Testament writings and the early liturgies are impregnated with
the passionate conviction that this world is *God's world*, and that
His Kingdom, inaugurated by Christ's life, death and resurrection, is being built up, in and through the Church, through the
action of the Holy Spirit, and will have a certain and glorious
End.

Early Christian worship was worship ' in the Spirit ', who is
the ' earnest ' of things to come, and the present power of God,
who always at the same time points forward to the glorious future
fulfilment of God's Eternal Purpose of Redeeming Love—the
re-creation of all things according to His will. It is ' in the
Spirit ' that we are able to worship; for it is He who makes the
Eucharist more than an external rite; He makes it a reality. It
is through Him that we are able to offer the ' sacrifice of praise '
and the offering of ourselves. In so doing, we are taking part
in an act which expresses the deepest meaning of sacrifice:
' the return of the creature to Him who made it for Himself, so
that it may find its end . . . in Him, and for His glory '.[2]

When, therefore, we ' proclaim the Lord's Death, till He
come ', we are joining with the whole Church, on earth and in
heaven, in praying that the whole world, and indeed, the whole

[1] I Cor. 16.22.   [2] E. Masure, *The Christian Sacrifice*, p. 41.

universe, may achieve this 'return' to God through sacrifice, when 'the creature makes the final act of casting itself into the Creator's arms'.[3] A modern French writer, Canon Masure, himself a Parisian, gives a vivid parable of this 'return', based on his own experience as a child, when he used to bowl his hoop in the Luxembourg Gardens: 'Do you remember', he writes, 'those wooden hoops which we used to throw ahead as children in the Luxembourg or in our own gardens, with a twist of the hand which brought them obediently back to our feet after a few yards' run? It seems that the whole Creation, cast by the Lord with a great sweep into space, as the Bible describes it, as Michael Angelo painted it, is controlled by an inner law to flow back towards its Creator, and the world of bodies, spirits and souls is a vast cycle of coming and going, in which God has His Glory, and creatures their happiness in Him.'[4] There is nothing easy or sentimental, however, in this thought of 'return' through sacrifice. Sacrifice demands the utmost effort of which we are capable: 'Sacrifice is the entire movement of our created nature'. To return to God, as He desires it, calls out all our energies; it is like 'the flight of the arrow to the mark'. And this entire surrender, this act of self-giving, is the moment at which man achieves his destiny. Yet all this effort on our part is a response to God's creative and renewing action on our souls. The 'End' to which He is leading us—and for which the whole world has been created—and the Hope with which He inspires us, is 'the gathering up of all things in Christ'.

Too often this supreme meaning of the Eucharist is either forgotten, or ignored. Many Christian people feel no need for sacramental worship, mainly because it seems to them to be divorced from real life. Others, however, who do communicate fairly regularly, are satisfied with an almost purely individualistic devotion. Yet all the time it has been true—and still is—that the aim of the Christian life, and of Christian worship, is not primarily the comfort and support of a certain number of individuals (though this may often happen), but the fulfilment of God's Purpose for the whole universe. For the Eucharist 'looks beyond every personal satisfaction to a more sublime objective. The transfiguration of all life, the unifying of body and soul, matter and spirit, by its redemption from egotism, and by total consecration to the purposes of God, is the special call and destiny of man. . . . For the Eucharist points back to the

[3] E. Masure, *The Christian Sacrifice*, p. 41.　　[4] Ibid., p. 42.

supreme sacrament of the Incarnation which discloses in visible
and temporal terms the nature of the Eternal God; and thus
declares the true significance of the Universe.'[5]   In the Eucharist,
as Evelyn Underhill insists again and again, 'the Church shows
forth . . . her great objective: the hallowing of the whole created
order and the restoration of all things in Christ'.[6]

This 'restoration of all things in Christ' means the rule of
God over every part and aspect of human life. It means that
nothing is outside His purpose or His power. The very fact
that in the Eucharist God uses material things, bread and wine,
to convey His life to us, means that our physical universe itself,
the whole economic basis of our life, is to be offered to God, that
in and through it He may accomplish His purpose for human
life: a 'new creation'.[7]   Our daily personal needs and our
special emergencies, all our relations with other people, the right-
ing of social wrongs, the healing of suffering minds and bodies,
the effort to achieve justice and wisdom and righteousness in
politics and in law; the consecration of all human gifts and
powers, from the simplest duties in home or hospital, shop or
factory, office or farm, to the responsible tasks of those men and
women called to lead and inspire others in Church and State, in
art, literature, and science: all this may—and should—be purified
and offered to God for His use. But the 'restoration of all things
in Christ' covers more than this: it embraces all the hidden
secret struggles, sufferings, prayers, and renunciations which
constitute the real 'life' of humanity. For it is God who incites
us to give, to suffer, and to adore; and He blesses, accepts and
uses all we offer. Nothing that is given to Him is ever wasted.

Thus present and future are blended as we pray with confidence, 'Come, Lord Jesus.' This sense of hope and expectation
of the total transformation of the whole created order is vividly
realized and expressed in the worship of the Eastern Orthodox
Church. This is how a modern Russian writer puts it:

'It is not only for the individual that the Sacrament of the
Lord's Supper has a central living mystic meaning, but for the
whole community, the whole Church, yes, for all mankind. For
here the divine mingles with the human, the terrestrial; here in
the Eucharist praise and sacrifice are offered to the Lord for the
whole world and by the whole world . . . and the whole cosmos
is hereby potentially ennobled and sanctified, in that earthly

---

[5] E. Underhill, *The Mystery of Sacrifice*, p. xii.   [6] Ibid., p. xiv.
[7] H. A. Williams, *Jesus and the Resurrection*, pp. 19ff.

elements of wine and bread become the glorified body and blood of the Son of God. That is why the idea of all creation assembled in spirit around the Eucharist altar so constantly recurs in the old liturgies of the East. For through Him, through His death and through the glorification of His Risen Body, here mystically represented, creation partakes of the glory of the redemption.'[8]

Too often this note of hope and exultation is absent from the sacramental worship of the West. Yet here, above all, we are called to rise above our daily anxieties and preoccupations to adore God, and to offer ourselves to Him for the coming of His glorious Kingdom. No one was more joyfully convinced of the hope of this fulfilment than St. Paul, yet no one has expressed more truly or poignantly what we feel about our present age, an age 'which has been twisted out of its true pattern': 'For we know that the whole creation groaneth and travaileth in pain together until now. And not only so, but ourselves also, which have the firstfruits of the Spirit, even we ourselves groan within ourselves, waiting for our adoption, to wit, the redemption of our body. For by hope were we saved.'[9]

The time in which we live: its disorder, its forgetfulness of God; its carelessness of human life; its cruelty and sin and oppression; its hunger and insecurity; for millions, its emptiness and meaninglessness; its sordidness, and fear, hatred and despair —fill us with a painful longing for a 'new heaven and a new earth, wherein dwelleth righteousness'. But sin and disorder do not only fill the 'world', but much of the life of the Christian Church is infected with the same evil spirit. Nowhere does this come out more clearly and painfully than in her disunity and divisions, above all at the Lord's Table. We have no right to come to that Table save as penitent sinners confessing our sins as a Church, and praying humbly and sincerely that Christ may lead us out of our disorder into the order and unity that He wills, and that He alone can create.

Yet the Eucharist is the Sacrament of hope. For our hope is in the Lord our God, who says to His People: 'Behold! I make all things new.' And we who feed on Christ in the Sacrament experience in ourselves 'the powers of the age to come'.

On the eve of His Passion our Lord was transfigured before His disciples, and manifested His Divine Glory. That ray of trans-

[8] Arseniew, *Mysticism and the Eastern Church*, p. 58.   [9] Rom. 8.22-24.

figuration . . . is not extinguished, but shines mysteriously in Christ's Sacraments; and all creation seeks and longs for it. The Sacrament, while it arises, and is realized within this world, also reaches out to the beyond. It is the prophecy and anticipation, and thence the realization of God as ' all in all ', in Whom the whole cosmos is destined to become a sacrament, and man's creative, divine-human calling to be fulfilled. . . . Into the midst of darkness gathering in a world weighed down by the burden of sin and suffering, is borne a faint yet unmistakable whisper, a call to the Wedding Feast of the Apocalyptic Lamb. And the parched and cracked lips of all creation cry, ' Come, Lord Jesus ! '[10]

O God, of unchangeable power and eternal light, look favourably on Thy whole Church, that wonderful and sacred mystery; and by the tranquil operation of Thy perpetual Providence, carry out the work of man's salvation; and let the whole world feel and see that things which were cast down are being raised up, and things which had grown old are being made new, and all things are returning to perfection through whom they took their origin, even through our Lord Jesus Christ. Amen

Holy, holy, holy is the Lord God, the Almighty which was and which is and which is to come. . . . Worthy art thou, our Lord and our God, to receive the glory and the honour and the power: for thou didst create all things, and because of thy will they were, and were created.

REVELATION 4.8-11

Great and marvellous are Thy works, O Lord God, the Almighty; righteous and true are Thy ways, Thou King of the Ages. Who shall not fear, O Lord, and glorify Thy name? for Thou only art Holy; for all the nations shall come and worship before Thee, for Thy righteous acts have been made manifest.

IBID. 15.3-4

Unto Him that loveth us, and loosed us from our sins by His Blood; and He made us to be a kingdom, to be priests unto His God and Father; to Him be the glory and the dominion for ever and ever. Amen.

IBID. 1.5-6

[10] E. Lampert, *The Divine Realm*, p. 139.

THE CHARACTER OF THE LAST SUPPER

THERE are four narratives of the Last Supper recorded in the New Testament: Matt. 26.26-30; Mark 14.22-25; Luke 22.15-20; I Cor. 11.23-26. The date and therefore also the character of the Last Supper is still being discussed by scholars. The problem is posed by the fact that in the three Synoptic Gospels (Matthew, Mark, and Luke) the Last Supper is regarded as the Passover Meal (Mark 14.12ff.); while in the Gospel of John it is clear that the author of this Gospel believed that the Last Supper took place before the Passover (John 13.1; 18.28; 19.14, 36). Some scholars (e.g. Dalman and Jeremias) regard the Supper as the Passover Meal; while others argue that this Supper was the 'Sabbath-Kiddush', or the sanctification of the Sabbath, when wine was blessed and bread was broken. This view is held by G. H. Box and others. On the other hand others (e.g. W. O. E. Oesterley, G. H. C. Macgregor, etc.) believe that this meal was the 'Passover-Kiddush', or the 'ritual sanctification of the Passover'. In neither instance, however, was it said that the meal was taken on a Thursday; this fact still forces us to assume that on this occasion an exception was made and the meal was eaten a day earlier than usual.[1]

Another theory (Lietzmann, Otto, etc.) is that the Supper was an ordinary Jewish religious meal, very like the formal supper of a *chaburah*, or a private group of friends. Such a group would meet each week for a special supper, usually on the eve of the Sabbath Day. Religious topics were discussed at such meals.[2]

These questions are of great interest, but their importance is often exaggerated. For whether the Last Supper was the Paschal Meal or not, the nearness of the Passover would be in the minds of all those who were guests at this Supper. The mind of Jesus Himself was evidently full of the thought of the Passover and its significance. The fact that Jesus suffered at the Paschal season; that during this Last Supper He was certainly thinking of the Passover (Luke 22.15);

[1] Vincent Taylor, *Jesus and His Sacrifice*, pp. 114-116.
[2] cf. G. Dix, *Shape of the Liturgy*, Chapter IV, and W. O. E. Oesterley, *The Jewish Background of the Christian Liturgy*.

and that in the Early Church He was called 'our Passover' (I Cor. 5.7), would naturally lead to the idea that the solemn remembrance of His Death was a 'Christian Passover'; this again may have influenced the Synoptists' accounts of the actual setting of the Last Supper.

In any case, it is clear that this final Supper, as recorded by the Synoptists, was of a special character. This group of friends may have felt that although they could not celebrate the Passover together, they could meet for this Last Supper. And 'if Jesus designed during the course of it to perform a solemn symbolical act with the bread and wine at the Table . . . then it is only likely that the "form" of this act would have a general likeness to existing religious practices at the Table.'

The account of the Last Supper in the Prologue of this book is based upon the following passages in the New Testament: Mark 9.33-37; Luke 22.24-27; John 13; I Cor. 11.24 (R.V.), and Mark 14.24. The Feet-Washing in John 13.1ff. does not interrupt a meal which has already begun. These Jewish religious meals followed very much the same pattern; often some preliminary food was served before the 'meal proper' began. It was after these 'relishes' had been served that the guests performed ablutions and special prayers were said. Then the meal itself began.

NOTE 2

THE WORD 'SACRAMENT'

THE Latin word *sacramentum* meant originally any thing or action or form of words which gave a solemn meaning to the thing, action, or form of words. Thus the money deposited by each of two litigants in a sacred precinct with a priest was called a 'sacrament'. The man who gained his suit got back his deposit. In its commonest use it means *the oath* which soldiers took, swearing that they would not run away or desert their post. Pliny uses the word in the same sense of *the oath* by which the Christians of Bithynia bound themselves at their solemn meetings for worship not to commit any wicked action.

Tertullian (*c.* A.D. 160-240) uses it in both senses: (*a*) of an oath of fidelity: (*b*) of the 'sacraments' of our religion, meaning, apparently, the Love Feast and the Eucharist. The word was used rather vaguely and broadly in Christian writings until the twelfth century.

Behind the word 'sacrament' there lies a blending of ideas and associations: on the one hand, there is the Latin word, with its associations with Roman law, but containing also a sense of something 'dedicated' or 'consecrated' or having a 'religious sanction'; on the other hand, in Christian Latin, from the third century onwards, the word was the accepted rendering of the Greek word mystery, or secret rite: it was also applied to objects of a symbolic character used in such rites. In the New Testament it almost always means a religious reality, long kept secret, but now revealed through Christ and His Church.

NOTE 3

SACRIFICIAL RITES

DURING these rites the choir sang:

'May this offering climb into space, and be known on high! May it obtain for us what we desire! I am come to this Mount, with my officers, to ask the August Heaven to grant earth the ripening of crops, a fruitful harvest.'

Then the Emperor again prostrated himself nine times, and the choir continued their chant:

'By my offerings I make my reverence known on high. May their smoke . . . rise aloft, and may blessing descend upon the people. That is what I, a little child (the Emperor), ask by these offerings.'

When the offerings had been consumed by the fire, the choir went on:

'The tripods and censers smoke, the pieces of flesh and silk are blazing, their smoke rises higher than the clouds, to show the pains of our people. May our music and our chants make known the devotion of our hearts.'[1]

All these rites bear witness to a deep desire for union with 'Heaven' or the 'gods', and a longing to win their favour. As

[1] Quoted by Canon Eugène Masure in *The Christian Sacrifice*, pp. 19-20, from the *Revue Illustrée de l'Exposition Missionaire Vaticane*, published officially August 15, 1924.

doctrine it is of course a vast mass of error—truth is found in its fulness in Christ alone—but 'if we take it as an expression of minds and wills in search of their end, it becomes the huge conflagration of a burning bush covering all the globe, with every tongue of fire a witness of adoration.[2] Indeed it is an anthropologist, at a scientific Conference on the Antiquity of Man, who comments thus on this universal, ancient, deeply rooted instinct for sacrifice:

'I believe that there always have been worshippers, suppliants, and lovers. . . . That has been enough for God. As the earth turns round the sun times without number, many crimes are committed on its surface, many shouts of grief and despair, even blasphemies, rise from this strangely fated planet to the horror-stricken skies; but the holy murmur from retreats where simple good men are praying, easily drowns the shouting and the blasphemy; and the smoke of sacrifice, a thin blue column rising into the calm air of dawn or dusk, bears a perfume so keen that it destroys the stench of crimes.'[3]

NOTE 4

SELF-EXAMINATION IN THE LIGHT OF THE BEATITUDES

THIS 'method' should be used in a free and positive way. For the Beatitudes describe the 'happy' life. In I Tim. 1.11 we read of the 'Gospel of the Glory of the Happy God', implying that 'the happiness of the Christian God consists in being a Redeemer'. To us the 'happiness' here suggested may seem a strange kind: Happy are the poor, the humble, the quiet and gentle people, happy too those who are dissatisfied with themselves and want to be better, who hunger and thirst for goodness; happy are the single-minded, those who are not distracted by self-seeking, who care for God and for other people; those who are always trying to make peace, wherever they are, who are compassionate and merciful in thought and word and deed, who suffer with others in their troubles, and willingly suffer for their own convictions. Each of these 'blessings' shows one element in the 'Christian style of life' which should be exhibited by those who

[2] E. Masure, *The Christian Sacrifice*, p. 24.   [3] Ibid., p. 26.

belong to Christ. This is life as it is meant to be lived here and now, in the midst of difficulties and hindrances of all kinds—and yet, a 'happy' life.

Blessed are the poor in spirit: i.e., those who are disciplined, detached, supple, obedient. Do I cling to things, habits or persons? Do I always want other people to fall in with *my* ideas? or am I willing to give up my own way (where no real principle is involved)? Do I find myself wanting to 'mould' people? children? friends? pupils? students? Am I possessive in my relationships? Do I want to 'get' something for myself rather than to 'give'? Do I use my gifts generously and unselfishly, without thought of praise or recognition?

Blessed are they that mourn: Am I truly sorry for grieving God? or am I only disappointed with myself? Do I really care about the sufferings and sorrows of other people? Am I trying to express understanding and practical sympathy with those in my own circle who need it?

Blessed are the meek: Do I even *want* to be 'meek'? or do I think it means being spiritless, weak, indifferent? I need to look at the 'meekness' of Christ: His courage, His controlled silence before His accusers, His acceptance of the Father's will to the utmost limits of human endurance—here we see what real 'meekness' demands: the elimination of self-will and self-centredness, using all our energies for God and for other people. . . . Am I 'meek' in this sense? or do I resent 'slights'? Do I long for notice? Do I mind what people say to me? Do I allow myself to brood over injuries whether real or imaginary? Am I sometimes stiff and disobliging? Do I yield gracefully when 'yieldingness' is required? or do I complain of 'frustration'? 'lack of scope'? or of the sins and faults of other people? Am I gentle in speech and manner?

Blessed are they that hunger and thirst after righteousness. What is this 'hunger and thirst'? It is a desire for simple goodness—a desire to be done with self-seeking, once for all, in every shape and form; such a desire is, at bottom, the desire for God. Do I want God like this? Do I long to see Him known and loved? Do I hate all evil and all injustice? Do I want to live in this deep desire to work with God to put things right that are wrong, in any way I possibly can?

Blessed are the merciful: This means that 'if we are to live as Christians then the whole world has to be our family, and all men our friends'. Do we want to live like this? Am I even willing to open my heart to everyone in the whole world, whatever their colour

or race or religion or lack of it, whatever their need? Am I full of
reverent pity for all who are outcast, sinful, lost, needy? and do I
try to do what I can to help? Do I ask our Lord to give me something of His own spirit of love and mercy?

Blessed are the pure in heart : That is, those who are single-minded,
who want only God and His will, who are quiet because they are not
thinking about themselves at all. Do I want to become single-minded?
Do I desire to desire God like this? ' What is more quiet than the
single eye? '

Blessed are the peacemakers : Do I ' make ' peace in my home? in
my place of work? in my work for social and religious causes? or am
I ' difficult '? Do people avoid me because I will not co-operate? I
need to have peace in my heart before I can make peace for others.
Christ is our Peace. In the Sacrament He gives Himself to us that
we may receive His peace, and then make peace in the world.

Blessed are the persecuted : Do I shrink from ridicule? Do I fear
the opinions of others, especially on matters of faith and principle?
Am I willing to be regarded as ' narrow-minded ' because I stand up
for the Christian Faith? Am I trying to be a faithful and courageous
witness where I am placed?

These are simply a few suggestions of the way in which such self-
examination might be carried out. In practice we shall inevitably
take a different line, according to our circumstances and duties. But
it is essential that such a method of preparation should lead on to
prayer for definite ' intentions ', suggested by the quality or command which has been the subject of our reflection. So that when we
come to the Lord's Table we come with a definite request that He
will give us out of the treasures of His own Risen Life, that element
which we most need: e.g., humility, courage, patience, single-minded-
ness, etc., but always as *His* gift, not as *our* effort.

We Christians having learnt the new blessings, have the exuberance of life's morning prime in this youth which knows no old age; in which we who are always growing to maturity in intelligence, are yet always young, always gentle, always new, for they must necessarily be new who have become partakers of the new world.

CLEMENT OF ALEXANDRIA

O God, who hast made all those that are born again in Christ to be a royal and a priestly race, grant us both the will and the power to do what Thou commandest; that Thy people who are called to eternal life may have the same faith in their hearts and the same piety in their actions.

Take away from us, we beseech Thee, O Lord, all our iniquities, and the spirit of pride and arrogance which Thou resistest, and fill us with the spirit of fear, and give us a contrite and humble heart, which Thou dost not despise—that we may be enabled with pure minds to enter into the Holy of Holies; through Jesus Christ our Lord.

Cleanse us, O Lord, from our secret faults, and mercifully absolve us from our presumptuous sins, that we may receive Thy holy things with a pure mind; through Jesus Christ our Lord.

We give thanks to Thee, O Lord God, Father Almighty, together with Thy Son our Lord God and Saviour Jesus Christ, and the Holy Spirit; and we offer unto Thee this reasonable service, which all nations offer unto Thee, O Lord, from the rising of the sun unto the going down thereof, from the North and from the South; for great is Thy Name in all nations, and in every place incense and sacrifice and oblation are offered unto Thy Holy Name.

LITURGY OF ST. MARK